For our parents, Ruthe and Milton Graff and Eric Durchholz, who have passed on, and for Annie Durchholz, who is still with us. They might not care to be associated with some of the stories in this book—or heck, even the title—but we love them anyway.

First published in 2012 by Voyageur Press, an imprint of MBI Publishing Company, 400 First Avenue North, Suite 300, Minneapolis, MN 55401 USA

The information in this book is true and complete to the best of our knowledge. All recommendations are made without any guarantee on the part of the author or Publisher, who also disclaims any liability incurred in connection with the use of this data or specific details.

We recognize, further, that some words, model names, and designations mentioned herein are the property of the trademark holder. We use them for identification purposes only. This is not an official publication.

Voyageur Press titles are also available at discounts in bulk quantity for industrial or sales-promotional use. For details write to Special Sales Manager at MBI Publishing Company, 400 First Avenue North, Suite 300, Minneapolis, MN 55401 USA.

To find out more about our books, visit us online at www.voyageurpress.com.

ISBN 978-0-7603-4230-5

Library of Congress Cataloging-in-Publication Data

Graff, Gary.
 Rock 'n' roll myths : the true stories behind the most infamous legends / Gary Graff and Daniel Durchholz.
    p. cm.
 Includes index.
 ISBN 978-0-7603-4230-5 (softbound w/ flaps)
 1. Rock music—Miscellanea. 2. Rock musicians—Miscellanea. I. Durchholz, Daniel. II. Title.
 ML3534.G72 2012
 781.6609—dc23
                    2011037351

Editor: Dennis Pernu
Design Manager: Cindy Samargia Laun
Cover and Interior Design: John Barnett/4 Eyes Design
Layout: K. K. Lemone

Printed in China

10 9 8 7 6 5 4 3 2 1

ROCK 'N' ROLL MYTHS

THE TRUE STORIES BEHIND THE MOST INFAMOUS LEGENDS

GARY GRAFF AND DANIEL DURCHHOLZ

Voyageur
Press

CONTENTS

IT'S A FAMILY AFFAIR

EAT TO THE BEAT

DOCTOR, DOCTOR, GIMME THE NEWS

ACROSS THE UNIVERSE

INTRODUCTION

Danny & The Juniors once sang that rock 'n' roll is here to stay, that it will never die.

The Philadelphia quartet was right about that—way back in 1958, when rock was still having its diapers changed. But the group could have added that rock 'n' roll will sometimes lie, too.

Oh, there are great truths told in rock and popular music. Think of the songs of Chuck Berry and Bob Dylan and James Brown. The Beatles and the Rolling Stones and Sly and the Family Stone. Bruce Springsteen and U2 and Pearl Jam. And that's just for starters.

But alongside the earnestness and enlightenment of great rock music is the personality of the movement, the larger-than-life dynamism that made and sustains it as a cultural force. It's a universe unto itself, casting a wider net than just songs on the radio or MP3s in your tablet or on your smartphone. It's a lifestyle and a life force, a fluid code that unites generations in thoughts, feelings, and philosophies and even creates ties that bind them to their predecessors in a manner that didn't happen with popular culture prior to rock.

It's Big, in other words, and when something makes that kind of footprint, it tends to spawn myths. And legends. And tall tales. It spins off stories of varying degrees of truth, from blatant falsehoods and ill-willed lies to kernels of actuality that are twisted and embellished into something better—or at least more provocative. And it doesn't matter if they're proven to be complete baloney because the sheer telling gives them a life of their own that exists alongside the "real" part of the story.

So there are probably people out there who believe that Robert Johnson and Led Zeppelin really did make deals with the devil. That Rod Stewart really did have his stomach purged of male sexual secretion. That Lady Gaga and Ciara are really part (or all, or formerly) male. That Paul McCartney really is dead and that the near-septuagenarian guy running around scoring ballets and playing Beatles songs in concert is the cosmetically altered stand-in who was put in his place in 1967. Or 1968. Or 1969—depending on which version of the story you believe.

While some of these and the other tales related in *Rock 'n' Roll Myths* are mean-spirited, there's a general sense of fun that comes with them as they're spread through the public. Whether true or not, they knock the artists down a peg or two and mitigate their outsized images with some flesh and blood. And a sly wink. Anyone who gets in the celebrity game, whether they're musicians, actors, politicians, or athletes, learns they need to have at least a bit of a sense of humor about themselves and embrace the circus and all of the sideshow acts that come with fame. Who's had more fun with Sting's reported tantric sexcapades, for instance, than Sting-a-ding-ding himself? And while it likely isn't the nicest thing to have the world believe that you had a candy bar eaten out of one of your lower orifices, when asked about the tale, Marianne Faithfull has always rolled her eyes with a sense of grace, drollery, and ladylike decorum.

The fifty-seven stories in *Rock 'n' Roll Myths* cover a wide range of artists and topics—birth and death, sex and murder, drugs and alcohol. There are hundreds more, of course, but we've chosen these fifty-seven for a variety of reasons, among them the notoriety of the artists, the sensationalism of the subjects, the depth of their impact, and their durability over time. We've also striven to make most of them fit mythic criteria. They are, for the most part, not true but have been spread for so long, and so far, that they continue to pop up and be accepted as fact, even when ample evidence has proven otherwise. Meanwhile, those that are true at their core—such as the fiery fate of Gram Parsons' corpse, Led Zeppelin's shark adventure, or Keith Richards snorting his father's ashes—have grown fantastically fanciful in their retelling, to the point where the mythological aspects are more readily accepted than the facts.

Through research and personal contact, we've tried to get to the bottom of each story and not only ascertain the truth but explain how these myths came to be and then came to be spread. Some remain mysteries; we're still not sure if John Lennon and Brian Epstein slept together or if Brian Jones was murdered, and Rod Stewart has never figured out how that rumor about his stomach contents started (nor have we). And those kinds of myths are, in some ways, the most fun.

So dive into the haze, purple and otherwise, with us. Hopefully you'll raise your eyebrows and drop your jaws—or at least get a few laughs. After all, it is only rock 'n' roll (with a few other genres thrown in), but we like it, like it, yes we do.

—Gary Graff and Daniel Durchholz

THE DEVIL INSIDE

CHAPTER 1

DID ROBERT JOHNSON SELL HIS SOUL AT THE CROSSROADS?

WHAT'S THE STORY BEHIND MISSISSIPPI'S VERY OWN FAUST?

Because rock stars covered his songs, seminal bluesman Robert Johnson gained far greater fame in death than he ever did in life. The Rolling Stones did "Love in Vain" on their classic 1969 album *Let It Bleed*. That same year, Cream, featuring Eric Clapton, performed "Crossroads" (which in Johnson's version was called "Cross Road Blues") on *Wheels on Fire*.

His songs "Dust My Broom" and "Sweet Home Chicago" became oft-covered blues and blues-rock standards as well.

But before it was reissued on the 1961 album *King of the Delta Blues Singers*, Johnson's music was largely unavailable and to some degree forgotten, though his legend lived on in stories told by other musicians who had known him, such as Son House, Johnny Shines, Henry Townsend, and Robert Junior Lockwood.

A few decades later—and more than half a century after his mysterious death—Johnson himself achieved rock-star status when *The Complete Recordings* box set sold half a million copies and won a Grammy Award. There is a story from that period that is too good not to be true. A clueless Columbia Records executive who was excited about the Grammy win suggested at a label meeting that a little press could only boost sales further. Couldn't this Johnson guy be made available for some phone interviews?

Alas, his music would have to speak for itself, which is pretty much the way it has always been. No other major figure in blues music—or perhaps

The 1961 posthumous Robert Johnson LP that launched a thousand bands. *Voyageur Press Collection*

ROBERT JOHNSON
KING OF THE DELTA BLUES SINGERS

All of the tracks mentioned at left give the distinct impression that Johnson was a man running both from the devil and toward him at the same time. The fabled crossroads is where they met, and while Johnson's "Cross Road Blues" doesn't specifically mention any sort of pact, his cries for mercy and salvation from God apparently go unheard, after which he moans, "Poor Bob is sinkin' down." In its own way, "Cross Road Blues" is the ultimate cautionary tale.

any genre—is as shrouded in myth as is Johnson. Little is known about his life, and much of what *is* known is subject to conjecture and contradiction. And his body of work, though slight—a mere forty-two tracks, including alternate takes—has been monumentally influential in terms of Johnson's stunning guitar technique; his emotional, sometimes scarifying vocals; and his songwriting, which left the impression that something—the past, a jealous lover or her husband, or perhaps the devil himself—was chasing Johnson and was not far behind. Even the details of his death and the exact location of his grave aren't known for certain.

Often, when the facts of life don't line up with what is known or seems plausible, the supernatural is brought into play. And so it was with Johnson, who was born out of wedlock, the eleventh child of a mother whose previous ten were fathered by her first husband. Early on, Johnson showed himself to be a ne'er-do-well, because, in his stepfather's words, "he wouldn't get behind the mule in the mornin' [and] plow."

Son House remembered him as "a little boy standing around" while House played gigs with fellow bluesmen Charley Patton and Willie Brown. During their breaks, Johnson would pick up their guitars and try to play.

"And such another racket you'd never heard," House said. "It made people mad, you know."

Johnson later disappeared for a while and when he returned, sat in once again, this time with a startlingly different result.

"So he sat down there and finally got started," House recalled. "And man! He was so good. When he finished, all our mouths were standing open. I said, 'Well, ain't that fast! He's gone now!'" Muddy Waters, witnessing a Johnson performance in Frye's Point, Mississippi, told the *New Musical Express*, "I got back in the car and I left because this was a *dangerous* man . . . and he was really *using* that guitar, man. . . . It was too heavy for me."

Bonnie Raitt, a student of the blues who was friendly with Son House and other Johnson contemporaries, recalled, "When they talked about him, they'd just shake their heads. I got the feeling they felt he was as hounded by the devil as everyone else does. It's hard to say what was real and what time has magnified or romanticized, but I do think it's backed up in talent. He's possessed when he plays."

Practice and hard work didn't seem a likely explanation for Johnson's sudden leap forward, simply because those weren't traits ever associated with him. Johnson was footloose and reckless in nearly all aspects of his life, especially in his relationships with women. As rapper turned roots rocker Everlast noted, "The legend of Robert Johnson is the beginning of the rock 'n' roll lifestyle."

"Did Robert really love?" Johnny Shines, one of Johnson's occasional

The king of the Delta blues singers, as honored by the U.S. Postal Service. *akva/Shutterstock.com*

traveling partners, once considered. "Yes, like a hobo loves a train—off one and on the other."

For some, the most plausible explanation for Johnson's otherwise unexplainable abilities was a deal with the devil—that he'd been given unsurpassed skills on the guitar in exchange for his immortal soul.

The particulars of such a transaction are understandably sketchy. But legend holds that one seeking such a deal would be playing guitar at the hour of midnight at a place where one country road crosses another. A large, black figure would appear, tune the guitar, and hand it back. Once the deal was done, the pact maker could play anything on the instrument that he could imagine.

However, Lockwood, whose mother lived with Johnson during the mid-1930s, says, "I don't know nothing about all that stuff. I think people were just jealous of the way he played and had to come up with a reason they weren't as good, so that was one of the stories they made up."

Once his skills kicked in, Johnson traveled far more extensively than most of his contemporaries. His recordings were made in Texas—in San Antonio in November 1936, and in Dallas the following June. But by the time he was sought out for a third session, and to play the famed From Spirituals to Swing concert at Carnegie Hall, Johnson's short life had come to an end at the age of twenty-seven.

Some say his death came at the hand of a jealous lover who poisoned him with a bottle of whiskey laced with strychnine. Or perhaps it was her husband who did him in. Some versions of the story embellish the tale, claiming that Johnson crawled on his knees and barked like a dog before he died. Still others say he was stabbed. In any case, it was a messy death, made more so in the minds of some as a means of the devil collecting his due.

Regardless of the vicissitudes of his life and death, Johnson's music is an unparalleled achievement. But the story of his alleged Faustian bargain completes a portrait of his artistry that can't be rendered with mere biographical details. Music historian Peter Guralnick has written, "Robert Johnson fulfilled in every way the requisite qualities of the blues myth. Doomed, haunted, dead at an early age; desperate, driven, a brief flickering of tormented genius."

Indeed, no other artist can send a chill down the spine quite like Johnson, who may have actually been a willing participant in the creation of his own myth with songs like "Cross Road Blues," "Hellhound on My Trail," and, most pointedly, "Me and the Devil Blues," on which he sang, perhaps presciently, "Early this morning when you knocked upon my door/And I said, Hello, Satan, I believe it's time to go." ✗

DID LED ZEPPELIN SIGN A DEAL WITH THE DEVIL?

THREE OF FOUR MEMBERS SOLD THEIR SOULS FOR SUCCESS. OR WAS THAT JUST THE RECORDING CONTRACT THEY SIGNED?

Jimmy Page knew he had something special in Led Zeppelin from the very first time he, Robert Plant, John Paul Jones, and John Bonham played music together. "It was just magical," the guitarist recalls. "It was very powerful. It was clear there was a special kind of chemistry at work, from the get-go, unlike anything I'd ever experienced before. We knew this could be very big."

But over the years, some have said Page sought a bit of outside help to ensure that success. Page and Led Zeppelin were not the first act reputed to have bargained with Beelzebub for personal gain; Robert Johnson and his supposed deal with the devil at the Mississippi Delta crossroads was well enshrined in music mythology by the time Page built Led Zeppelin from the ashes of the Yardbirds. In this case, Page and all his mates except Jones, according to the tales, signed a blood-ritual pact to trade their souls in exchange for Zeppelin's climb up the stairway to rock 'n' roll heaven.

And the quartet's phenomenal start in 1969—a one-two punch that took its self-titled debut album to No. 10 on the Billboard charts, with *Led Zeppelin II* reaching No. 1—made it look like Satan was living up to his end of the bargain.

The deal, however, is something Page and others in the Zep camp have steadfastly denied over the years, and there's never been any sort of "proof" brought forward by its proponents. Jason Bonham, the son of the late Zep

A salute to the prince of darkness? Probably not.
Mick Gold/Redferns/ Getty Images

drummer John Bonham (and an occasional Zep drummer himself), calls the story "a bit of a far-fetched thing. . . . There was a lot of success and tragedy in Led Zeppelin, when you think about it. But, you know, I wouldn't say the deal with the devil thing was anything, and I've been around the boys long enough to know."

Richard Cole, Zep's longtime road manager, weighed in as well, pooh-poohing the "demonic curse . . . that would ultimately lead to the deflating of the Zeppelin" in his memoir *Stairway to Heaven: Led Zeppelin Uncensored*: "To my knowledge, no such pact ever existed. Jimmy was a great one for spinning yarns. . . . But despite Jimmy's preoccupation with the supernatural, he rarely discussed his dabbling in the occult with the rest of the band. One of our roadies once said to me, 'I tried to broach the subject once, and Jimmy went into a rage. I'd never raise the issue again.'"

Much of the Satanic rumor stemmed from Page's expressed interest in the occult in general and particularly in the life and doctrines of Edward Alexander "Aleister" Crowley, a British mystic and, some say, black magician who dabbled and experimented in sex, hedonism, drugs, philosophy, and psychology—and who Page called "a misunderstood genius of the twentieth century." Crowley's tenet, "Do what thou wilt" (a motto for libidinous rock stars everywhere), was inscribed in the run-off grooves of the *Led Zeppelin III* album, while Page's "ZOSO" symbol on the band's fourth album incorporates elements found in the Zodiac and in books about alchemy. Page also owned an occult bookshop and publishing house, The Equinox, during the early 1970s, and one of its works was a reprint of Crowley's 1904 edition of the occultist text *The Book of the Goetia of Solomon the King*.

For a time Page even owned Boleskine House, a Scottish estate where Crowley lived from 1899 to 1913 and where he did some of his most crucial writings. Page sold the house around 1991 and filmed his fantasy sequence for Zep's 1976 concert film, *The Song Remains the Same*, in which he portrayed The Hermit from a tarot card deck, on a nearby mountainside. But Jason Bonham recalls asking Page about the house: "I said, 'Have you been there?' and [Page] goes, 'I went once. It kind of freaked me out.' I never imagined him being that guy, anyway. When you see him with children, he's just way too sweet. He's not that guy."

Led Zeppelin's run of tragedies—the Plant family's near-fatal car crash in August 1975 on the Greek island of Rhodes, the death of Plant's son Karac in 1977, and John Bonham's death in 1980, which effectively ended the band—were further interpreted as signs that Page's dabblings came with a dark, heavy price. After Bonham's death in particular, British tabloids widely theorized about a supposed "curse" on the group. There were unconfirmed reports that Page could be heard speaking in tongues behind the walls of his house in Windsor, England, after Bonham died there on September 25.

But Page dismissed it all as bilge. "I don't see how the band would merit a karmic attack," he argued. "All I or we have attempted to do is go out and really have a good time and please people at the same time." He lamented to road manager Cole that "People take my interest in the occult and give it a life of its own."

But Page was also aware that a little bit of darkness put some weight behind the hammer of the gods. "If they want to believe all the rumors, let them," he told Cole. "A little mystery can't hurt." ✖

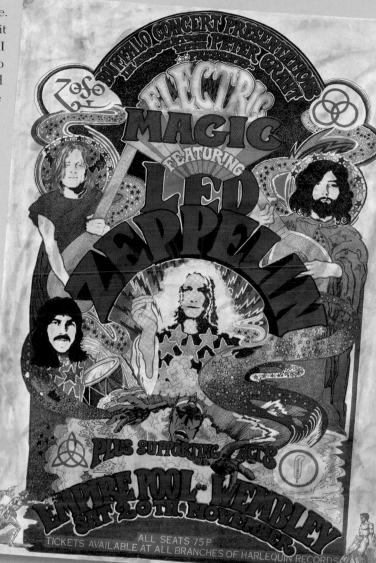

This 1971 concert poster would certainly seem to indicate a "preoccupation with the supernatural."
Voyageur Press Collection

MYTH TRACK

The song "Houses of the Holy" was, ironically, not included on the 1973 Zep album that bore the same name but rather was held back until 1975's *Physical Graffiti*. It became a fan favorite but never worked its way into the group's live show during the original foursome's run.

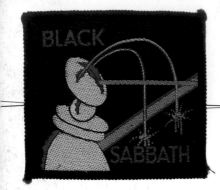

CHAPTER 3

HOW DID SABBATH GET THEIR BLACK ON?

WERE MEMBERS OF THE TRAILBLAZING METAL BAND SATANISTS? AS ALWAYS, THE DEVIL'S IN THE DETAILS.

Back off, you Satanists. Can't you see Black Sabbath is trying to get some religion? *Michael Ochs Archives/ Getty Images*

Under the indisputably heavy, but sadly generic name Earth, four English punters—guitarist Tony Iommi, singer John "Ozzy" Osbourne, bassist Terence "Geezer" Butler, and drummer Bill Ward—aspired only to be a pub-rocking blues outfit like the Peter Green–era Fleetwood Mac.

But when the band started rehearsing in a movie theater where horror movies drew lines around the block, inspiration struck.

"Isn't it strange how people will pay money to frighten themselves?" Osbourne, writing in his autobiography, *I Am Ozzy*, recalls Iommi saying. "Maybe we should stop doing blues and write *scary* music instead."

Which they did. With a riff that sounds like it could have been dredged from the bottom of the River Styx, plus spooky lyrics about being Satan's "chosen one," the song "Black Sabbath" made a big enough impression on Earth's audiences that the title, which Butler cadged from Mario Bava's 1963 film starring Boris Karloff, became the band's new moniker.

More evil-sounding music would follow. "Look into my eyes, you'll see who I am/My name is Lucifer, please take my hand," Osbourne howls on "N.I.B." (by some accounts an abbreviation for "Nativity in Black," natch). Other songs dealt with unspeakable evils—death, nuclear annihilation, drug abuse, mental illness—as well as the requisite demons. Sabbath's album covers contained images of graveyards, inverted crosses, even demonic possession. It pretty much went without saying that the band's souls belonged to the Dark Lord.

So, to paraphrase Woody Allen, how did we misread those signs?

"I can honestly say that we never took the black magic stuff seriously for one second," Osbourne declares. "We just liked how theatrical it was."

As did Sabbath's audience, whose devotion in the form of album purchases placed all of the band's early records high on the charts, though critics by and large reviled their shtick. ("Bubblegum Satanism," sniffed Nick Tosches in his bizarre 1971 *Rolling Stone* review of *Paranoid*.)

Occultists took it seriously, though, and followed the band wherever they went.

"They just wouldn't fuck off, those Satanists," Osbourne wrote in his memoir. "I'd walk out of my hotel room in the morning, and they'd be right outside my door, sitting in a circle on the carpet, all dressed in black hooded capes, surrounded by candles."

Osbourne drew the ire of his admirers by walking up to the candles one day and singing "Happy Birthday" and blowing them out.

As for their own spell-casting abilities, "We couldn't conjure up a fart," Osbourne told *Rolling Stone* in 1978. "People think we're into black magic and voodoo, which we never have been. A lot of that had to do with the initial drive to sell the band. We created a brand, if you like, a package. But I hope the coffin has been bolted forever on that black magic thing." ✗

MYTH TRACK

They may have been pretend Satanists rather than the real thing, but if you didn't know that, you'd have a hard time distinguishing "Black Sabbath"—the opening cut on the band's 1970 self-titled debut album—as anything but an audio documentary of a soul being drawn down into Hell by ol' Beelzebub himself. Gnarly!

CHAPTER 4

KISS: SATANIC ACRONYM OR DIVINE INSPIRATION?

KNIGHTS IN SATAN'S SERVICE? HELL, THEY'RE NOT EVEN DUKES OF DEMONOLOGY.

Not long after New York band Wicked Lester became KISS—and the rest of the world started to get a look at this quartet of glam-cum-hard rockers, with their makeup and blood-spitting, fire-breathing theatrics—rumor began to spread that the new name was as much an acronym as a moniker.

KISS, it was said, stood for either Knights in Satan's Service or Kids in Satan's Service. Either way, Satan seemed to be a believable svengali for a group that sang about drinking "Cold Gin" and getting a "Deuce" from their women, and who, of course, wanted to "Rock and Roll All Nite"—and party every day. Some also pointed out that the S's in the KISS logo looked like a Nazi SS insignia (they're actually intended to look like lightning bolts).

Bassist Gene Simmons—he of the long tongue and aforementioned fire-breathing and blood-spitting—acknowledges that he had a hand in starting the Satanic misperception.

In his 2001 autobiography, *Kiss and Tell*, Simmons (who was born Chaim Weitz in Israel), writes, "This rumor started as a result of an interview I gave in *Circus* magazine after our first album; in response to a question, I said that I sometimes wondered what human flesh tastes like. I never wanted to really find out, but I was curious intellectually. Later on, this comment seemed to ignite the whole idea that in some way KISS was aligned with devil worship."

And, Simmons added, he saw no reason to set things straight: "When I was asked whether I worshipped the devil, I simply refused to answer for a number of reasons: the first reason, of course, was that it was good press. Let people wonder. The other reason was my complete disregard

for the people who were asking. Through the years, whenever religious fanatics accosted me, especially in the southern states, and quoted the Old Testament at me, I would quote them back chapter and verse. They didn't know that I had been a theology major in school."

So read his—and his band mates'—lips: KISS does *not* stand for anything in Satan's Service. "That's ludicrous," co-founder Paul Stanley noted, "but we had a lot of laughs about it. And it didn't hurt, you know? It created an aura of mystery around us, and mystery sells."

Lips actually had something to do with how KISS really became the band's name. It was an idea drummer Peter Criss tossed out after the group had decided to move on from Wicked Lester, and it got his band mates thinking. "One day Paul and Peter and I were driving around, brainstorming for new names," Simmons writes. "At one point—we were stopped at a red light— Paul said, 'How about KISS?' Peter and I nodded, and that was it. It made sense. . . . Since then people have talked about all the benefits of the name: how it seemed to sum up certain things about glam rock at the time; how it was perfect for international marketing because it was a simple word that people understood all over the world. But we just liked the name, and that was that."

The proof is in the proverbial pudding, of course. Since 1974, KISS has sold more than 100 million albums worldwide and remains a top concert attraction as well as a merchandising juggernaut that feeds its KISS Army fan club with everything from licensed condoms to coffins. "We get you coming and going," Simmons likes to say. ✖

Gene ponders the taste of Paul's flesh, London, 1974.
Peter Cade/Hulton Archive/ Getty Images

Satan, you say? If you're going to talk about KISS and ol' Beelzebub in the same breath, better do it while playing "Hotter than Hell," the title track from the group's sophomore album and second release of 1974.

CHAPTER 5

IS SLAYER SYMPATHETIC TO THE REICH?

ONLY IN THE "EYES OF THE INSANE," HEAVY METALERS SAY.

Any metal band worth its mullets gets accused of devil worship or Satan sympathies at some point of its career. Certainly Slayer, one of heavy music's Big Four (along with Metallica, Megadeth, and Anthrax), is viewed in that light. That's what happens when you sling around album titles like *Hell Awaits*, *God Hates Us All*, and *Christ Illusion*. It's part of the gig.

But another association has dogged the quartet throughout its thirty-plus-year career: that of being neo-Nazis.

This particular rumor dates back to the early days of Slayer's career, specifically to its classic 1986 album, *Reign in Blood*, and even more specifically to that LP's opening track, "Angel of Death." Written by guitarist Jeff Hanneman, the blistering 4:51 song deals with Nazi doctor Josef Mengele and his horrific experiments on prisoners of the Auschwitz death camp during World War II. Hanneman, an acknowledged collector of Nazi memorabilia and the son of a World War II vet who was part of the 1944 D-Day invasion in Normandy, France, told *Decibel* magazine that the lyrics were inspired by two books he read about Mengele during one of Slayer's tours: "I thought, 'This has gotta be some sick shit.' So when it came time to do [*Reign in Blood*], that stuff was in my head."

But Hanneman has always contended that "Angel of Death" in no way glorifies Mengele or his work: "I know why people misinterpret it," he told KNAC.com. "It's because they get this knee-jerk reaction to it. When they read the lyrics, there's nothing I put in the lyrics that says necessarily he was a bad man because to me—well, isn't that obvious? I shouldn't have to tell you that."

Nevertheless, the song touched a nerve with Jewish and Holocaust-survivor organizations, which were also unnerved by Slayer's logo: an eagle (part of Nazi imagery), as well as an S whose typography resembled the insignia of the Third Reich's SS corps. Columbia Records, which distributed Slayer's label, Def Jam, refused to put out the album because of its overall lyrical themes and graphic artwork, so *Reign in Blood* (whose producer, Rick Rubin, is Jewish) was ultimately released by Geffen Records—although that company decided not to list it on its official schedule.

Not Nazis, so stop asking! Slayer's Kerry King and Jeff Hanneman, 2009. *haak78/Shutterstock.com*

The controversy did not dilute the song's impact, of course. Both *Reign in Blood* and "Angel of Death" are considered metal classics. And Hanneman was not deterred from dipping into his Nazi interests again for "SS-3," a song about the SS's Reinhard "The Hangman" Heydrich that appeared on the group's *Divine Intervention* album in 1994.

Slayer, meanwhile, continues to repel any suggestions of Nazi sympathies within the band. "You kind of sit there dumbfounded, like how can we have ties to the Nazis?" says bassist and vocalist Tom Araya. "We've got a Cuban drummer [Dave Lombardo, who was born in Havana] and a Chilean singer and bass player: two people who would've been in the gas chambers if the Nazis got a hold of us. So how can we be Nazis? It's so ridiculous. We don't really ignore it, but we kind of let it go and eventually you hope people stop asking and figure it out. It happens a lot less now, but you still hear it once in a while. And what more can you say—No! We're not [Nazis]." ✗

MYTH TRACK

It's dark, frightening, audacious—everything that a song about a villainous, psychopathic mass murderer should be. In the world of thrash, though, we expect to be a little scared, too, and "Angel of Death" will certainly make anyone think twice about glorifying the Holocaust.

CHAPTER 6

DOES MARILYN MANSON DANCE WITH THE DEVIL?

IS THE FLORIDA SHOCK ROCKER A SATANIST? ANTICHRIST IS MORE LIKE IT.

It's pretty easy to peg someone whose breakthrough album is titled *Antichrist Superstar* as a Satanist, as is the case with Marilyn Manson. And, oh yeah, he's an ordained minister in the Church of Satan. But as Paul Harvey would say (though probably never about Manson), wait 'til you hear the rest of the story.

From the outset, Manson's plan for world domination was based on calculated outrage. "As a performer, I wanted to be the loudest, most persistent alarm clock I could be," he wrote in his autobiography, *The Long Hard Road Out of Hell*, "because there didn't seem like any other way to snap society out of its Christianity- and media-induced coma."

In other words, he did it for us—which, if you think about it, is ironically a pretty *Christian* thing to do.

In his quest, Manson targeted the usual hot-button issues: sex, drugs, violence (he's *for* them, of course), and religion, which he considers one of the roots of all evil.

And if you're looking to set off alarms in the latter category, Satan is the go-to guy.

Manson, whose real name is Brian Warner, was raised Episcopalian, though his father was Catholic, and he attended a nondenominational Christian school. While living in Ohio, he even attended a few services conducted by televangelist Ernest Angley. He rebelled against his upbringing, though, and quickly developed a taste for the darker side of religion.

As Marilyn Manson, he became known for ripping up Bibles at his concerts (in Utah he opted for the Book of Mormon), and his concerts were constantly under siege by protesting Christian groups.

Manson paid a few visits to the San Francisco home of Anton LaVey, founder of the Church of Satan and author of the Satanic Bible, whom he came to regard as a father figure. When LaVey made him a minister in the church, Manson seemed somewhat indifferent to the, um, honor. "It seemed then (and it still does) that my ordainment was simply a gesture of respect," he wrote. "It was like an honorary degree from a university."

Ultimately, Manson's version of Satanism, as writer Anthony DeCurtis has pointed out, is more akin to the radical individualism of Friedrich Nietzche or Ayn Rand than it is to devil worship. "It's not about ritual sacrifices, digging up graves, and worshipping the devil," Manson wrote in his book. "The devil doesn't exist. Satanism is about worshipping yourself, because you are responsible for your own good and evil."

"I'm not and have never been a spokesperson for Satanism," he added. "It's simply part of what I believe in, along with Dr. Seuss, Dr. Hook, Nietzsche, and the Bible, which I also believe in. I just have my own interpretation." **✗**

MYTH TRACK

What else could we pick here but "Antichrist Superstar," the title track of Marilyn Manson's second studio album? It's not just the song itself, which is heavy with the dread and foreboding of lines like "The angel has spread its wings/The time has come for bitter things." Admittedly, that might suggest more than a bit of Satanic content. But its inclusion here is based on the way Manson traditionally performs the song in concert (and in the song's as-yet-officially-unreleased video), replete with fascist, Nuremberg Rally–style imagery. He's clearly going for more of a secular thing here. Of course, should he rip pages out of a Bible during the song, as he sometimes does, that's something else again. But Manson doesn't have a problem mixing his messages, so long as the combined effect is one of effrontery and outrage.

CHAPTER 7

DID ALICE COOPER COMMIT FOWL PLAY?

SOME SAY THE SHOCK ROCKER KILLED A CHICKEN ONSTAGE IN TORONTO—A BILLION-DOLLAR BABY OF A STORY IF THERE EVER WAS ONE.

The Toronto Rock and Roll Revival festival, held September 13, 1969, featured a heady lineup, including John Lennon (with Yoko Ono and an all-star Plastic Ono Band) in his first full-fledged concert apart from the Beatles, plus the Doors, Chuck Berry, Chicago, and more. The show's headlines, though, were made not by these heavyweights, but by one of the lesser-known acts: Alice Cooper, which killed a chicken during its set.

The fowl play, however, was not premeditated and was, in fact, accidental. But it created a legend that became an intrinsic part of the macabre theatricality that helped establish the group as a rock 'n' roll juggernaut.

The group, which had formed during the mid-'60s in Phoenix, Arizona, was signed to Frank Zappa's Straight Records label for its first two albums: 1969's Zappa-produced *Pretties for You* and the post-Toronto *Easy Action* in 1970. The quintet wasn't getting much traction on the West Coast, however, so it decided to relocate temporarily to Detroit, where frontman Cooper (née Vincent Furnier) was born and still had family, and where it felt audiences might be more receptive.

Alice Cooper's spot on the Toronto bill, according to Cooper himself, was locked in by co-manager Shep Gordon, who helped the festival organizers put the show together. Rather than accepting a fee for his work, Gordon requested that they slot Alice Cooper on the bill between the Doors and

Finger-lickin' good. Alice Cooper takes a break from the usual chicken dinner. No, he didn't kill it himself. *Gijsbert Hanekroot/ Redferns/Getty Images*

Lennon, ensuring a large crowd and a level of prestige greater than the group had earned at the time.

The Cooper group, meanwhile, had already started making theatrics part of its shows. "We kinda liked the idea of experimenting with anything we thought would blow people's minds," guitarist Michael Bruce wrote in his 1996 memoir, *No More Mr. Nice Guy: The Inside Story of the Alice Cooper Group*. That included wearing makeup (which you can do when your frontman goes by a woman's name), singing behind screen doors set up on stage, and using a variety of props.

At one point during the height of the "Paul (McCartney) is dead" rumor in 1969, bassist Dennis Dunaway appeared on stage in a dark suit and barefoot—just like McCartney on the Beatles' *Abbey Road* album cover—while the band played "Lay Down and Die Goodbye." Another regular trick: slashing open pillows and then using CO_2 to blow the feathers around the stage. Cooper even recalled Lennon and Ono expressed liking that stunt when they met in Toronto: "It was performance art to them," he wrote in his autobiography, *Alice Cooper, Golf Monster*.

What happened in Toronto has never been in question. Somehow a live chicken got loose on stage around the middle of the Alice Cooper set. Cooper was a bit surprised but played along; "I didn't know how it got there," he remembered, "but I picked it up and just threw it away from the stage. It had wings; I thought it would fly. I'm a Midwestern boy, y'know—a big-city kid. I'd never lived on a farm or anything. I didn't know chickens couldn't fly."

Instead, the bird plummeted into the front of the crowd, where it was torn to pieces by fans. The mainstream press, still not supportive of the youth counterculture or rock 'n' roll, had a field day with the story, running photos of Cooper tossing the chicken and publishing stories that claimed it was a ritual slaughter and that the singer drank its blood. It made international news—which was great news, according to then–label boss Zappa.

As Cooper writes in *Golf Monster*: "Frank Zappa phoned me. 'Alice, did you really kill a chicken?' 'Not exactly.' I told him my side of the story. 'Well, don't tell anybody! Everybody hates you—that means the kids will love you.'" Thus was born a legend that Cooper says is "still one of the first questions people ask me today."

But while Cooper "never understood where the heck a live chicken came from in the first place at the time," it turned out he had to look no further than his own manager. According to Cooper, while he was writing *Golf Monster*, Gordon "finally confessed. Shep was the man behind the chicken incident!" But Gordon apparently didn't hide the fact from everybody, even on the day of the show.

According to Bruce, the band had stopped using the pillow-hacking trick, especially in clubs where owners didn't like the mess. So in Toronto, he wrote, "we decided, rather than feathers, let's throw chickens out. Why not use the real thing? It was a camp inside joke." Nobody expected Cooper to throw the chicken off the stage, however. "I don't know if he was that naïve or not. When was the last time you saw a chicken fly by your window? But of course once the chickens [*Note the plural, which is not in any other accounts of the incident. –Au.*] had landed, whatever happened to them in the audience we didn't have anything to do with." Bruce also contended that Cooper's account that "the people in wheelchairs . . . were more insane than the other fans" was "embellished."

The Alice Cooper Band would go on to use even more elaborate stunts on stage, including mock beheadings, hangings, and electrocutions, as well as dismembering baby dolls, cavorting with live snakes, and dancing with giant teeth. With 1971's *Love It to Death* and its hit single "I'm Eighteen," the audience would also start to catch on, starting a run of four consecutive platinum albums, hit singles ("Be My Lover," "School's Out," "No More Mr. Nice Guy") and, of course, sold-out shows.

Cooper, who's been a solo act since 1975, hasn't mellowed with age, either; during the group's Rock and Roll Hall of Fame induction in 2010, he made his acceptance speech in a blood-splattered tuxedo with a snake draped over his shoulders. But the only chicken that night was on plates in the Waldorf-Astoria Hotel ballroom. **✗**

Offstage, Alice Cooper (the man) is a pleasant, Christian-minded, charitable citizen who is indeed the *Golf Monster* of his memoir's title. Turn on the spotlights, though, and he becomes the "Killer" of the seven-minute title track from the group's 1971 album, which went platinum and was, at No. 21 on the Billboard charts, its highest-charting release to that point.

MYTH TRACK

CHAPTER 8

WAS BRIAN JONES' DEATH AN ACCIDENT—OR MURDER?

SOME BELIEVE THE STORY OF THE STONE'S "DEATH BY MISADVENTURE" IS ALL WET.

Rolling Stones co-founder Brian Jones' July 2, 1969, death in the swimming pool at his home—Cotchford Farm in East Sussex, England, once owned by Winnie the Pooh creator A. A. Milne—has become both myth and mystery. Ruled "death by misadventure" at the time, it was long suspected to have been murder and, since 2009, is now a reopened police investigation.

It's been recounted in several books, including one by Jones' girlfriend at the time, and is the subject of the 2005 biopic *Stoned* by British filmmaker Stephen Woolley. The trail includes shoddy police work, accused accomplices, late-arriving witnesses, a killer who purportedly confessed on his deathbed, and, somewhere in all this, a rock band that had booted Jones out just weeks before he died and whose principal members didn't even attend his funeral. It's an epic tale, and it hasn't been definitively concluded.

It also placed Jones at the head of the "27 Club," a cluster of rockers who died at the very same age (see sidebar).

Lewis Brian Hopkins Jones was in a rather public decline at the time of his death. He'd formed the Rolling Stones in 1962, placing an ad in London's *Jazz News* looking for fellow musicians to form an R&B band with him, and was the group's leader in its early days. But his role diminished over time thanks to drug use, interpersonal conflicts, and a mercurial temperament. Band mates Mick Jagger and Keith Richards, a.k.a. the

Future head of the 27 Club, Brian Jones. *Peter Francis/ Redferns/Getty Images*

Glimmer Twins, became the group's chief songwriters and creative forces, and Richards even ended up with Jones' girlfriend, Anita Pallenberg. Jones' musical contributions were also becoming less crucial to the Stones, and a second drug bust, in May 1968, put him at risk of being denied a U.S. work visa, threatening the Stones' planned tour in 1969.

Matters came to a head while the group was recording its *Let It Bleed* album in the spring of 1969. Jones' participation was erratic, and the band was becoming resentful. Richards, by all accounts, played nearly all of the guitars on the album, with Jones contributing percussion on "Midnight Rambler" and autoharp on "You Got the Silver." Jagger reportedly even warned Jones that if he didn't turn up for the May 21 photo shoot for a new compilation album, *Through the Past Darkly (Big Hits Vol. 2)*, he'd be fired. Jones was there—but his days in the band were still numbered.

The Stones had already brought in new guitarist Mick Taylor by June 9, when Jagger, Richards, and Stones drummer Charlie Watts visited Cotchford Farm, where Jones was living with his Swedish girlfriend Anna Wohlin, to deliver the news he was out. Jones was reportedly given an upfront severance as well as an annual stipend for as long as the Stones remained together. He was also allowed to make the announcement that he was leaving the group, making it look like his decision rather than his band mates': "I no longer see eye-to-eye with the others over the discs we are cutting," he said in a statement. So the Stones rolled on, and Jones rolled alone.

Jones was plotting a few musical moves, even chatting up the Beatles' John Lennon about a collaboration, but mostly he was a homebody, busying himself with drugs, Blue Nun wine, and renovating Cotchford Farm. He hired Frank Thorogood, who'd also done work for Richards, to oversee the home improvements, but Thorogood, who was seventeen years Jones' elder, and his crew disliked the effete rocker and by some accounts often taunted him. The contractor, who had moved into an apartment over the estate's garage, was particularly peeved when Jones rebuked him after a support beam fell during dinner on July 1, and threatened to withhold payments and review some of his previous bills. But Jones subsequently apologized and invited Thorogood to go swimming with him on the evening of July 2.

It was, by Wohlin's account in her 2001 book, *The Murder of Brian Jones*, a tense night, with a taciturn Thorogood—who was married, but accompanied by a nurse named Janet Lawson—cool to Jones' friendly overtures. In the pool, Jones, an avid swimmer, tried to be playful, pulling Thorogood under the water by his ankles. Thorogood retaliated by dunking Jones, who took it in a spirit of good fun.

What happened next is where the mystery begins. Wohlin was called back to the house for a phone call, and during the conversation she heard Lawson screaming for her to return to the pool—where she found

Jones "lying spread-eagled on the bottom," unconscious. She called for Thorogood—whom she had passed in the kitchen, lighting a cigarette, on her way out of the house—to come and help. He took his time, she felt, and acted impassively ("cold as ice") as he slipped into the pool to pull Jones' body out. Wohlin and Lawson administered CPR until an ambulance arrived, but Jones was declared dead.

The coroner ruled the incident "death by misadventure," but many have felt there was more to the story, focusing on the moments after Wohlin was called away for her phone call. No traces of drugs and just a quantity of beer were found in Jones' body, and though he'd placed an inhaler by the side of the pool in case of an asthma attack, Wohlin wrote that Jones did not need it that night.

Cotchford Farm, the site of Jones' "death by misadventure." *Jim Gray/ Keystone/Hulton Archive/ Getty Images*

Robert Johnson: d. August 16, 1938, in Greenwood, Mississippi; possibly poisoned by a jealous husband or lover.

Alan "Blind Owl" Wilson (Canned Heat): d. September 3, 1970, in Los Angeles; barbiturate overdose (possible suicide).

Jimi Hendrix: d. September 18, 1970, in Kensington, Greater London; sleeping pills overdose/asphyxiated on his own vomit.

Janis Joplin: d. October 4, 1970, in Los Angeles; heroin overdose.

Jim Morrison: d. July 3, 1971, in Paris; unknown causes.

Ron "Pigpen" McKernan (Grateful Dead): d. March 8, 1973, in Corte Madera, California; gastrointestinal hemorrhage (due to alcoholism).

Pete Ham (Badfinger): d. April 24, 1975, in Surrey, England; suicide.

Gary Thain (Uriah Heep, Keef Hartley Band): d. December 8, 1975, in England; drug overdose.

Chris Bell (Big Star): d. December 27, 1978, in East Memphis, Arkansas; car accident.

D. Boon (Minutemen): d. December 23, 1985, in Tucson, Arizona; van accident.

Pete de Freitas (Echo & the Bunnymen): d. June 14, 1989, in England; motorcycle accident.

Kurt Cobain: d. April 5, 1994, in Seattle, Washington; self-inflicted gunshot wound.

Kristen Pfaff (Hole, Janitor Joe): d. June 16, 1994, in Seattle, Washington; heroin overdose.

Mia Zapata (The Gits): d. June 16, 1994, in Seattle, Washington; murdered.

Richey Edwards (Manic Street Preachers): February 1, 1995 (missing); officially presumed dead November 23, 2008.

Bryan Ottoson (American Head Charge): d. April 19, 2005, in North Charleston, South Carolina; prescription drug overdose.

Amy Winehouse: d. July 23, 2011, in Camden, London; accidental alcohol poisoning termed "death by misadventure."

Photo Combi Press

Wohlin believes that Thorogood drowned Jones while she was away. She wrote that Thorogood warned her against implicating him in Jones' death, telling her, "The only thing you need to tell [the police] is that Brian had been drinking and that his drowning was an accident. You don't have to tell them anything else." In her book, Wohlin also claims that Thorogood, who died in 1993, signed a deathbed confession for Stones chauffeur Tom Keylock, something Keylock has denied, and the document has never surfaced. In his 1994 book, *Paint It Black: The Murder of Brian Jones*, author Geoffrey Giuliano related Thorogood's words to Keylock: "It was me that did Brian. I just finally snapped. It just happened."

Meanwhile, A. E. Hotchner, who wrote the early-'90s Stones book *Blown Away*, found two people who felt they had seen Thorogood kill Jones and two other men who were presumed to be part of the construction crew. Jones' pal Nicholas Fitzgerald and another friend claimed to have arrived at Cotchford Farm at about 11 p.m. that night for a visit and saw one of the men holding Jones' head under the water. In their account, the nurse, Lawson, was also standing by the pool as it happened. Fitzgerald and his companion were driven off by one of the other men by the pool. Hotchner later tracked down one of the crew, identified in the book as "Marty," who claimed that even more people—wives and girlfriends of the workmen— were there to witness the killing. He claimed that the entourage simply meant to harass Jones but "got carried away," though he added, "I wouldn't say what happened was an accident."

Wohlin also wrote that the Stones' press agent, Les Perrin, became involved in the postmortem, offering to pay her in order to stand mute about Jones' death and not grant any interviews. She openly questioned whether the Stones organization was trying to protect Thorogood, but could not guess why. A number of items were stolen from Cotchford Farms after Jones' death, including furniture, musical instruments, and, rumor has it, some recordings he was working on.

The messy affair came to a kind of rest in the following week. The Stones dedicated their free concert on July 5 in London's Hyde Park to

Jones, where Jagger read the Percy Bysshe Shelley poem "Adonais" and attempted to release two thousand white moths. Unfortunately, many had died in their boxes prior to release or did die shortly thereafter on an oppressively hot day. Jones was buried on July 10 in Cheltenham Cemetery in a casket contributed by Bob Dylan. Jagger and Richards did not attend the funeral.

Speculation as to what happened has never ceased. Several books, including Wohlin's, continued to muse on what really happened that night by the swimming pool. Meanwhile, the continuing media investigations did bear some fruit. In August 2009, Sussex police announced they were reopening the case, trolling through, among other things, six hundred documents journalist Scott Jones had gathered during four years of research for a story published in November 2008 in the *Mail on Sunday* newspaper. Among them was a fresh account of the incident by Lawson, who claimed she saw Thorogood jump into the pool and "do something to Brian" that she felt killed the musician—an account supported by Albert Evans, the first police officer on the scene. Scott Jones' investigation also revealed that three unidentified witnesses were allowed to leave the scene without being questioned and that Joan Fitzsimons, a former girlfriend of Thorogood's, was attacked three weeks after Jones' death because she was planning to speak to the media about Thorogood's involvement. Fitzsimons died in 2002, without ever making a public statement. ✖

MYTH TRACK

Given the tragic circumstances and continuing mystery surrounding Brian Jones' death, the Rolling Stones' 1966 hit "Paint It, Black" seems an appropriate tone-setter. Not only is its mood appropriately bleak, but it also features one of Jones' finest contributions to a Stones track, a sitar riff that gives the trippy, swirling tune an exotic, Eastern flavor.

WHY WAS PAUL McCARTNEY (TEMPORARILY) DEAD IN 1969?

THE WORLD DIDN'T WISH MACCA DEAD IN 1969. SOME PEOPLE JUST THOUGHT HE MIGHT BE.

The rumor that rocked Beatles fans worldwide had its roots in Detroit, where Russ Gibb, a disc jockey at WKNR-AM began broadcasting the infamous "Paul is dead" rumor, pointing to numerous clues that confirmed the sad truth and professing that McCartney had been replaced by a cosmetically altered look-alike. "I'll forever be known as the Great Ghoul. I buried Paul," Gibb said in later years, with a laugh.

McCartney, at least, found some humor in it. During a 1989 press conference in New York City, he cracked that "Paul's dead. We know that for a fact. I'm just a double." At a similar gathering in Chicago, he broke into a wry grin when he told reporters, "It was another rumor. I didn't believe that one."

Gibb, however, felt there was enough credibility to start the rumor in the first place.

But while Gibb is roundly credited with spreading the "Paul is dead" rumor, he doesn't claim to have started it. In fact, researchers have traced its origins to a fantasy article written by a student at an unspecified Midwestern university (kind of like a *Penthouse* Forum letter, right?). Gibb was alerted to it during his regular weekend air shift on October 12, 1969. The call came from a university student in Ypsilanti. A writer for the *Michigan Daily*, he heard the rumor through the college media grapevine and passed it on to a skeptical Gibb.

"I said, 'I've heard that every rock star is dead or is a doper or has sexual preferences that are different,'" Gibb remembered. "I sort of dismissed it, but he said, 'Wait. Have you played 'Revolution No. 9' backwards?'"

That piqued Gibb's interest; played backward, the song from *The Beatles* (a.k.a. "The White Album")—an experimental exercise in recording

Macca keeps an eye on the death rumors. *Fiona Adams/ Redferns/Getty Images*

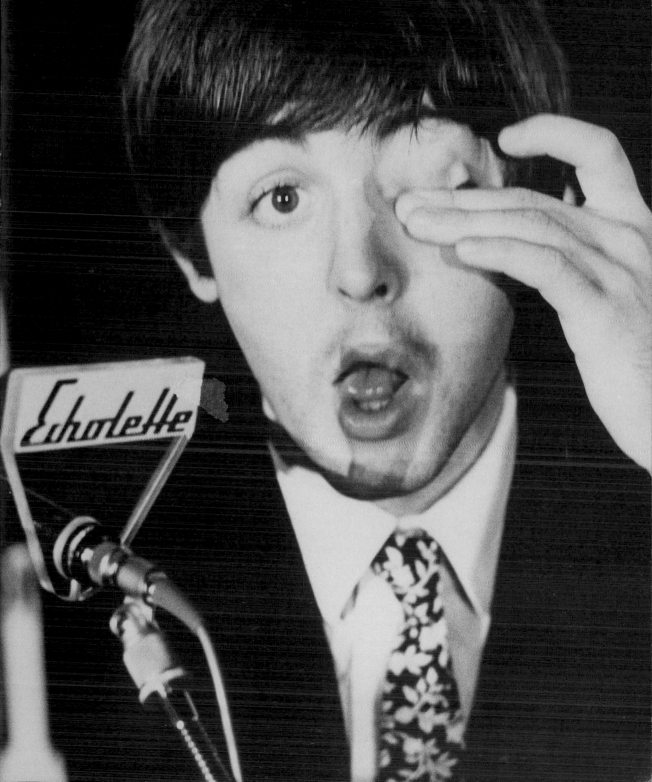

techniques—contains the distinct line "Turn me on, dead man." And Gibb put it on the air. "Immediately after that, the phone started to light up," Gibb recalled. "The phones just went crazy."

Gibb also put in a call to a friend, superstar guitarist Eric Clapton, in London. Clapton had played on sessions with the Beatles and was friendly with each of the band members. He laughed when Gibb asked him about the rumor.

"Then I said, 'Well, have you seen [McCartney] recently?'" Gibb added. "And he said, 'Come to think of it, I haven't seen him around.' The way he said it is what really flipped all of us out. It was just this small inkling that maybe there was something to this.

"Within two hours, we were getting calls from around the country, and kids were giving us the clues," Gibb said. "The wire services were calling. I got a call from *Time* magazine. Kids from here were calling their friends in Toledo and wherever, and they were calling their radio stations. By that night, it was everywhere." (Of course, in these Internet-dominated days, one can only imagine that what took hours in 1969 would take mere minutes, or perhaps even seconds, to go viral today.) Those clues the kids were phoning in included:

- If you play the Beatles' hit "Strawberry Fields Forever" backward, you hear John Lennon chanting "I buried Paul."
- The cover of the *Sgt. Pepper's Lonely Hearts Club Band* album depicts McCartney's funeral, with the Beatles surrounding his freshly dug grave.
- When the song "Revolution No. 9" from *The Beatles*, a.k.a. "The White Album," is played backward, you can distinctly hear John Lennon saying "Turn me on, dead man."
- The cover of the then new *Abbey Road* album was said to show a funeral procession; the four Beatles are walking across the street, and McCartney—or his stand-in—wears no shoes, symbolizing the fact that he was dead.
- On the same album cover, McCartney is out of step with his band mates, and a license plate on a nearby Volkswagen reads "28 IF," implying McCartney's age *if* he were alive. (Actually, McCartney was twenty-seven at the time.)

If things were chaotic at WKNR, it seemed like the world was suddenly coming to an end at the London headquarters of Apple Corp., the Beatles' company. When Gibb finally reached Derek Taylor, the Beatles' PR man, he screamed, "What does a man have to do to prove he's alive? He's alive! That's all you have to do."

In his 1983 book, *The Love You Make*, former Apple executive Peter Brown recalled that "the Apple switchboard in London was deluged with calls. None of us found the rumor at all amusing, and we very sternly assured all the callers that Paul was alive, in good health, and enjoying himself." But Brown and his Apple cohorts would not reveal McCartney's whereabouts, and McCartney wouldn't emerge from his farm in Scotland to quell the rumors.

Obviously, that kept said rumors on high flame. Gibb was among a number of disc jockeys and reporters who flew to England to try to track down McCartney, to no avail. All the while, the beleaguered Beatle refused to give in and confirm his whereabouts.

He was eventually flushed out by a team of reporters from *Life* magazine who traveled to Scotland and tromped around McCartney's farmland until he confronted them with a temper tantrum and doused them with a bucket of water. Minutes later, according to Brown's book, he chased after them and made a deal: The *Life* entourage gave him the film of the tantrum, and he allowed them an exclusive interview and photos of his family.

"The rumors of my death have been greatly exaggerated," McCartney, quoting Mark Twain, told *Life*. He wryly added, "However, if I was dead, I'm sure I'd be the last to know."

The rumor had its benefits. Gibb enjoyed a brief moment of international renown and sales of Beatles records picked up. Gibb, who also owned Detroit's famed Grande Ballroom concert club, recalled that Bhaskar Menon, chairman of EMI Music Worldwide, Apple's parent company, called to express his gratitude: "He said, 'I just want to thank you. Their records were slacking off about then. You've cleared the warehouse of Beatles stock before Christmas.'"

Gibb says Menon also sent him a complete collection of Beatles albums in appreciation. ✘

Oh, go ahead—slap on the experimental sound collage "Revolution No. 9" from "The White Album" and see if you can hear the "Turn me on, dead man" part. And if you sync the song up just right with Pink Floyd's *The Dark Side of the Moon* . . .

MYTH TRACK

CHAPTER 10

HOW DID GRAM PARSONS' CORPSE COME TO BURN IN THE DESERT?

THE COUNTRY–ROCK PIONEER NEVER BURNED UP THE CHARTS, BUT WHEN HIS MANAGER TORCHED HIS BODY, HE TURNED THE TROUBLED SINGER'S STORY INTO THE STUFF OF LEGEND.

Gram Parsons' infamous
Nudie suit celebrated some
of his favorite things.
*Jim McCrary/Redferns/
Getty Images*

Gram Parsons said he had a vision of "cosmic American music." It was country music at its core, with pathos-laden tales of heartbreak sung in high, honeyed harmonies. But its attitude was pure rock 'n' roll, as was Parsons' troubled personal life, which was filled with sex, drugs, and a taste for misadventure.

Parsons' music has been cited as the fount of the country-rock and alternative-country genres, and that alone likely would have guaranteed him a place in music history. But for good or ill, it is his death by overdose and the subsequent theft and burning of his corpse by his road manager that have made an indelible impression on anyone who hears of it.

"There isn't a better exit than the early death while you're still beautiful, and then the strange afterlife of the corpse being dragged into the desert," R.E.M. guitarist Peter Buck said in Gandulf Henning's Parsons documentary film, *Fallen Angel*.

The scion of a wealthy Florida family, Parsons was playing in rock 'n' roll cover bands during his teen years, often in clubs owned by his stepfather, Robert Parsons. He later attended Harvard, but left during his first year.

Leaving Harvard, Parsons had an eye toward becoming a folk singer, but his intentions changed dramatically due to his newfound obsession: country music. He formed the International Submarine Band in New York, but moved to Los Angeles, where the group recorded *Safe at Home*, often cited as the first country-rock album.

Freak scene. Parsons (far right) unwinds with the Burritos, 1969.
Jim McCrary/Redferns/ Getty Images

By the time it was released, however, the band was history. Parsons joined the Byrds, where his influence swayed the band to record the country-flavored classic *Sweetheart of the Rodeo*. But he left the band when his new friend, Rolling Stones guitarist Keith Richards, convinced him it would be unethical to tour South Africa, then subject to an international boycott because of the country's policy of apartheid.

Chris Hillman thought Parsons' political high-mindedness was just a dodge to cover his real reason for not going: he wanted to hang out with Richards. "I think [Parsons] was really climbing that ladder and we were just one of the rungs in the ladder he was going up," the Byrds bassist later said.

But Hillman took the next step up that ladder *with* Parsons, forming the Flying Burrito Brothers and recording such country-rock classics as "Hot Burrito #1" and "Sin City" for their debut album, *The Gilded Palace of Sin*. After a sloppy, booze-and-drug-soaked tour (on which they traveled by train, no less) and one more album—*Burrito Deluxe*, which featured the first release of the Stones song "Wild Horses"—Parsons quit the band.

The Burritos' records were not commercially successful, but the group cut an iconic figure thanks to the distinctive Nudie suits its members wore. In *Fallen Angel*, Nudie protégé Manuel Cuevas pointed out that the design of Parsons' suit was actually prescient: "What he was transferring to me in terms of ideas for making the suit was the actual way that he wanted to die, from the flames to the cross to the marijuana to the pills and to the girls."

After the Burritos, Parsons retreated to Villa Nellcôte, Richards' mansion on France's Côte d'Azure, where the Stones were recording *Exile on Main Street*. The friendship between the two deepened as they bonded over obscure country records and controlled substances. Returning to the States, Parsons recorded his solo debut, *GP*, which prominently featured the harmony vocals of a young singer Hillman had alerted him to: Emmylou Harris. They toured and later recorded the tracks that would become Parsons' second solo album, *Grievous Angel*.

All the while, his personal life was a mess. He'd fathered a child with Nanci Lee Ross, a girl he'd stolen from David Crosby. He later married a young actress, Gretchen Burrell, and their relationship was tempestuous. His relationship with Harris, meanwhile, whether platonic or something more, has mostly been a closed subject with her.

Parsons became estranged from his stepfather, who he'd learned was implicated in the death of his mother. He split from Burrell and moved in with his road manager, Phil Kaufman. When Byrds guitarist Clarence White was killed by a drunk driver, Parsons attended his funeral and was appalled by the straight-laced affair. He informed Kaufman that if he were to die, he wanted no part of a similar ceremony. Instead, he wished to be cremated and his ashes spread in Joshua Tree National Forest, his favorite retreat. Kaufman agreed to comply.

Just before a scheduled fall tour, Parsons traveled to Joshua Tree with a girlfriend, Margaret Fisher; his assistant, Michael Martin; and Martin's girlfriend, Dale McElroy. Though not using heroin at the time, Parsons' partying got out of control, and he likely overestimated his tolerance for other opiates. He overdosed on morphine and died in a hotel room on September 19, 1973.

The various stories about his death conflict on essential details. Even the medical reports disagree: The coroner's report said Parsons died of a heart attack, which the hospital report blamed on the alcohol content in his body. The autopsy, meanwhile, cited drug toxicity.

But all of that was mundane compared to what happened next.

Informed of his stepson's demise, Bob Parsons made arrangements for the body to be flown from Los Angeles International Airport to New Orleans for interment there. Recalling his pact with Gram, however, Phil Kaufman had other ideas.

Borrowing a hearse owned by McElroy, Kaufman and Martin fortified themselves with booze and drove to LAX, where they claimed the body, saying the Parsons family had changed its mind about the arrangements and wanted it transported to another airport. Kaufman signed a release form using the name "Jeremy Nobody."

Throughout the years, Kaufman has embellished his version of the story with one-liners and various details that can't be confirmed, giving the entire episode the cast of an oft-told tall tale.

On their way to Joshua Tree, for example, Kaufman said in *Fallen Angel* that he and Martin stopped at a gas station. "We filled the hearse with regular and filled a container up with high-test," Kaufman said. "The high-test was for Gram. We didn't want him to ping."

Ba-dum-bum.

Arriving at Cap Rock, a popular destination for LSD enthusiasts, they opened the casket, poured the gas in, and set Parsons' body aflame. And while it may be true that their intentions were pure—they simply wanted to carry out their friend's wishes, after all—the fact that they left his still-smoldering remains behind (the next day campers reported a "burning log" to authorities) gives the story a macabre and unsavory twist.

Aside from Kaufman, who has made a cottage industry of his act—he wrote a book, *Road Mangler Deluxe*, which was turned into an execrable movie, *Grand Theft Parsons*, starring Johnny Knoxville—most of Parsons' friends and all of his relatives were revolted by his body's desecration.

Kaufman and Martin were arrested and charged with misdemeanor theft—not because they stole a body, mind you, but because they stole *a coffin*. They pleaded guilty on what would have been Parsons' twenty-seventh birthday and paid a fine of $300 each, plus $708, the casket's replacement value.

To raise money, they held a benefit party for themselves at Kaufman's house, where they charged admission to see the featured entertainers, including disc jockey Dr. Demento, Bobby "Boris" Pickett (of "Monster Mash") fame, and—completely incongruously—protopunk outfit the Modern Lovers featuring Jonathan Richman. Kaufman designed custom beer-can labels, reproduced on T-shirts, that said "Gram Pilsner: A Stiff Drink for What Ales You."

Undoubtedly, Kaufman's irrational act put a crazy coda on Parsons' short, tragic, and recklessly tossed-away life. But he left a lot more behind than only that.

"People should know his music," Emmylou Harris said in *Fallen Angel*. "That should be his legacy, not the way he died." ✖

MYTH TRACK

Gram Parsons' legend and legacy were such that he's had a host of songs written about him, including John Phillips' "He Had That Sweet Country Sound," Poco's "Crazy Eyes," Johnny Rivers' "Artists and Poets," and more recently Emmylou Harris' "The Road." Our choice, though, is "My Man," by Bernie Leadon, who played with Parsons in the Flying Burrito Brothers. Leadon sang the song with his post-Burritos group, the Eagles, whose stratospheric success owes an enormous debt to Parsons' pioneering "cosmic American" country-rock sound.

CHAPTER 11

IS THAT THE SOUND OF MURDER ON "LOVE ROLLERCOASTER"?

DEATH ON THE ROLLERCOASTER OF LOVE? WHAT A SCREAM!

Some groups, it's said, are willing to die for their art. Or kill for it.

The latter was the case with the Ohio Players and their 1975 hit, "Love Rollercoaster."

The legend behind the song is that the high-pitched, terrified scream heard just before the 2:30 mark on the single, and just after it on the *Honey* album version, is the real sound of a woman being killed. The actual circumstances, meanwhile, are the subject of several variations:

- The most common is that it's Ester Corbet, the model on the cover, who's seen dipping herself—provocatively—in honey, both on the front and in the inner gatefold. Supposedly the honey was heated in order to make it easier to pour, but it burned her skin. And then it hardened, further disfiguring her when she removed it. When she returned to the studio later and threatened to sue the band, she was stabbed by (a) the Ohio Players' manager, (b) a band member, or (c) an engineer, and that her scream was recorded and looped into the song.
- Another says it was one of the band members' girlfriends who happened to be in the apartment (!) where the song was being recorded and was murdered by an intruder.
- Some spreading the tale say it was a cleaning woman in either the aforementioned studio or apartment who was killed while the band was working on the song.
- There's also a theory that it was a real scream taken from a 911 tape.
- Or, some have said, it's taken from a mental institution recording of a shock therapy or primal scream session.

Ester Corbet on the infamous *Honey* gatefold.
Voyageur Press Collection

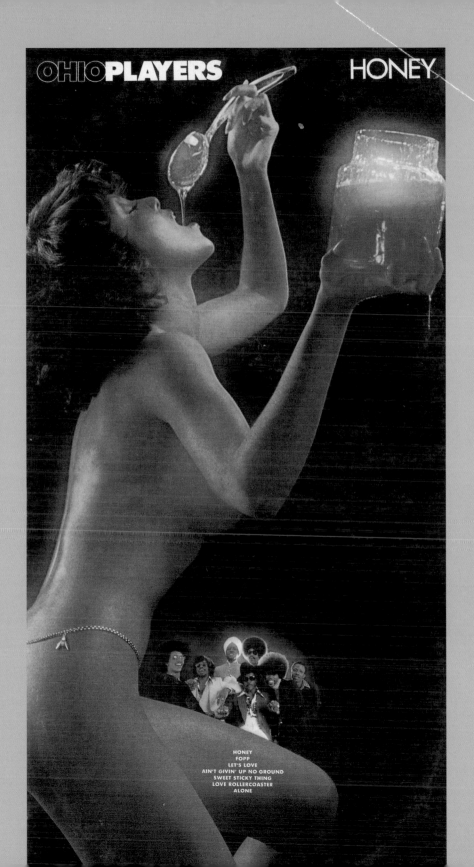

In all cases, Billy Beck should consider himself flattered.

Beck was the Ohio Players' keyboardist at the time of the recording, and it's him—not even a woman—who performed the scream to simulate the thrills 'n' chills of going down the big dip of a rollercoaster. Drummer Jimmy "Diamond" Williams, who leads the current incarnation of the group, says that Beck was "trying to do one of those big diva-type screams, like Minnie Riperton or Mariah Carey did." But, Williams notes, the band decided that the murder myth was worth encouraging. "It got people talking about the song who might not have paid attention to us otherwise," he says, "so we just kind of shut up and let it hang out there."

It's impossible to say who started the myth, but it got a national airing when Casey Kasem reported it on his syndicated radio show, *American Top 40*, while the song was ascending the charts in early 1976. "Love Rollercoaster" rode to No. 1 on the Billboard Hot 100 (the group's second chart topper) and on the R&B Songs chart (its fourth). It also took the *Honey* album to No. 2 on the Billboard 200 and the top of the R&B Albums survey.

"Love Rollercoaster," meanwhile, has had a long ride beyond being a golden oldie. The Red Hot Chili Peppers recorded a version of it in 1996 for the animated film *Beavis and Butt-Head Do America*, and it has been featured in other movies, such as *Final Destination 3* and *Urban Legend*, and in the Nintendo Wii video games *Boogie* and *Rock Band*.

"It's good when you've been blessed to write songs that people have great memories of," Williams says. "It was a great period of time. There were some incredible artists out there and some incredible writers, and we just wanted to stay with the flow of being good musicians and good writers, too. And now we have songs like 'Love Rollercoaster' that we can perform and give a chance for the people and ourselves to reminisce about some times that were a little better and when we were a little younger." **X**

What a scream. The Ohio Players' Leroy "Sugarfoot" Bonner onstage, 1976. *Colin Fuller/ Redferns/ Getty Images*

MYTH TRACK

We assure you that if you listen to "Love Rollercoaster," whether the Ohio Players' original (especially the longer album version) or the Red Hot Chili Peppers' killer cover, you'll need more than honey to put out the fire when you start burning up the dance floor.

DID SID VICIOUS' MUM SPILL HIS ASHES?

PUNK ROCKER'S EARTHLY REMAINS RESTING IN PEACE—WHEREABOUTS UNCERTAIN.

The Sex Pistols' Sid Vicious was a punk-rock prototype, living hard and fast, dying young (at twenty-one), and leaving a . . . well, the disposition of that corpse, much less its appearance, is somewhat in question.

Vicious' body was cremated; we know that much. Where the ashes wound up is the issue. The most authoritative accounts place them at the Philadelphia grave of Nancy Spungen, the girlfriend who preceded him in death by nearly four months. But there have long been adamant claims, coming from the likes of Sex Pistols' manager Malcolm McLaren, New York Dolls guitarist Johnny Thunders, and fellow musician Neon Leon, that Vicious' mother, Anne Ritchie Beverley, accidentally spilled his ashes at London's Heathrow Airport, although there's disagreement about whether that occurred in the arrivals lounge, on the concourse, or on the airport tarmac.

And some even contend that because of the accident, Vicious' ghost still haunts the Heathrow environs.

The ashes debate is just part of a nearly four-month nightmare of death, murder allegations, drug overdoses, and suicide attempts. The Sex Pistols were long over, having broken up January 17, 1978, following a shambolic U.S. tour, by October 12 of that year, when Vicious (real name John Simon Ritchie) found the twenty-year-old Spungen, a Philadelphia native he'd been dating for nearly two years, dead in the bathroom of their Chelsea Hotel room in New York City from a single stab wound to her abdomen. Vicious, who owned the knife that was used in the killing, was charged with second-degree murder and freed on bail. McLaren lined up famed attorney F. Lee

Sid Vicious on the Sex Pistols' shambolic U.S. tour. San Antonio, Texas, 1978. *Richard E. Aaron/Redferns/ Getty Images*

Bailey to represent Vicious in the case and helped raise money for his defense by selling T-shirts that read "I'm Alive. She's Dead. I'm Yours." in his London clothing shop. Vicious was also planning to record with Sex Pistols mates Steve Jones and Paul Cook in order to raise more cash for the case.

On October 22, Vicious attempted suicide and was admitted to Bellevue Hospital in New York. Upon his release, however, he was arrested again on December 9, this time for attacking Patti Smith's brother, Todd Smith, with a beer bottle during a Skafish concert at Max's Kansas City in New York. He spent fifty-five days in Rikers Island prison—where his mother, according to photographer and friend Eileen Polk, would sneak him heroin—and was released on bail on February 1, 1979.

He celebrated his freedom at a party that night at the New York apartment of his new girlfriend, Michelle Robinson. Vicious scored some heroin, partly with the help of his mother, and overdosed at one point, only to be revived. After he and Robinson retired for the night, however, Vicious passed away in his sleep. An autopsy showed that the heroin solution he took was of a lethal purity—estimates range between 80 and 99 percent—and that he had essentially drowned in his own fluids. Legend has it that a note found afterward in his pocket confirmed that he and Spungen "had a death pact, and I have to keep my half of the bargain. Please bury me next to my baby in my leather jacket, jeans and motorcycle boots. Goodbye."

Cremation—which was chosen because, according to Polk, no funeral home wanted the notoriety of a Sid Vicious ceremony—ensured that such a burial would never take place. So did Spungen's family, who wanted nothing to do with their daughter's alleged killer or his family. And King David Cemetery in Philadelphia, where Spungen was buried, is a Jewish graveyard that was unlikely to allow a gentile who was not a spouse to be interred there.

Polk, however, told Legs McNeil and Gillian McCain in their book, *Please Kill Me: The Uncensored History of Punk*, that Vicious' ashes never left the country. Rather, after the Spungen family rejected Beverley's pleas to spread his ashes by Nancy's grave, Beverley, Polk, and some other friends went to King David ostensibly to pay their respects at Nancy's grave but actually planning to disperse the ashes there. A couple of cemetery escorts did not leave them alone, however, so Polk says she and Beverley resorted to Plan B: "We drove around to the other edge of the cemetery. We parked the car and Anne took the ashes, went over the fence, back to the gravesite, and dumped Sid's ashes on Nancy's grave. Then she came back and got in the car and said, 'Well, they're finally together.' And that was that."

Polk's account has never been formally documented, and Beverley, who died in 1996, never set the record straight. So if you're ever at Heathrow and spot a spiky-haired ghost with a Fender Precision bass dangling off his left shoulder, you'll know which story really has legs. ✖

Sid and mum, 1978. *Daily Express/Hulton Archive/ Getty Images*

MYTH TRACK

For a summation of Vicious' short but eventful life, look no further than his cover of the Heartbreakers' "Born to Lose," which appears on *Sid Sings*, an album released some eight months after his death. It features mostly live covers of songs by the Monkees, the Stooges, Johnny Thunders, the Sex Pistols, and more. As bleak as it is energetic, it's a perfect way to remember the doomed punk rock provocateur.

13

DID BOBBY MCFERRIN DO HIMSELF IN?

DON'T WORRY . . . REALLY.

In the fall of 1988, singer Bobby McFerrin was on top of the music world. His song "Don't Worry, Be Happy," a bouncy ode to the power of positivity, became the first a cappella song to climb to No. 1 on the Billboard Hot 100. The following spring, he took top honors at the Grammy Awards, winning Record of the Year, Song of the Year, and Best Male Pop Vocal Performance.

But the song was a fluke, a novelty hit that threatened to overshadow a career built on musicality, innovation, and the singer's four-octave vocal range. His 1984 album, *The Voice*, for example, was a tour de force solo performance, recorded without overdubs or accompaniment—the first of its kind released by a major label. "I'll tell you, if I ever have a hit, it's going to be by accident, it's not going to be because I tried," he once vowed.

And so it was: a simple melody, a whistled intro, a few words snagged from Indian mystic Meher Baba, sung in a Jamaican accent over an a cappella reggae riddim, and—*Bang! Zoom!*—McFerrin was king of the world.

For a little while, anyway. But during that time, it seemed as if McFerrin and the song—to say nothing of its goofy video, featuring the antics of McFerrin, Robin Williams, and noted clown and actor Bill Irwin—were *everywhere*. In terms of the pop universe, though, McFerrin's reign was brief. Whether it was because of his quick return to relative obscurity, revenge for the song's puerile lyrics and unsurpassable earworm quotient, or because some people simply enjoy a story with a sick twist, rumors began to circulate that the singer who advised "In every life we have some trouble/When you worry you make it double" had topped himself. Not in the sense of having a bigger hit or winning more Grammys, but rather, in the British sense.

In other words, he'd killed himself.

Bobby McFerrin sings it "note for note," 2011. *haak78/Shutterstock.com*

Obviously, the rumor was false. However, it's highly likely that anyone who sat through the song a few too many times in a row has at least given suicide and/or murder a passing thought.

For his part, McFerrin decided to stop performing "Don't Worry, Be Happy" in concert to avoid being pigeonholed. But he used the creative freedom it had purchased to light out for more ambitious musical territory, releasing increasingly experimental works such as 1990's *Medicine Music* (recorded with his ten-member a cappella "Voicestra") as well as projects featuring Yo-Yo Ma and Chick Corea. He later became the creative chair of the St. Paul (Minnesota) Chamber Orchestra and conducted symphony orchestras throughout North America and Europe.

"Don't Worry, Be Happy" is forever accorded a place in the firmament of pop's one-hit wonders. But McFerrin remains definitively above ground, following his muse wherever it takes him and perhaps even following his own feel-good advice. ✖

MYTH TRACK

If you've heard "Don't Worry, Be Happy" once, you've heard it a million times. Or perhaps it just feels that way. Rather than recommending McFerrin's unlikely breakthrough hit, we invite you to check out the sort of thing he's excelled at for years—something like "Blackbird," a solo a cappella cover of the Beatles' tune from his 1984 album, *The Voice*. It's guaranteed to create the kind of laid-back, carefree mood that "Don't Worry" only talks about.

14

WAS JOHNNY THUNDERS' DEATH MORE THAN JUST JUNKIE BUSINESS?

THE PUNK ROCKER'S FATAL DRUG OVERDOSE WAS EASY ACTION— BUT WAS THE EXPLANATION TOO EASY?

There was great sadness but not a great deal of surprise when former New York Dolls guitarist Johnny Thunders was found dead at New Orleans' St. Peter's Guest House on April 23, 1991, at the age of thirty-eight. After all, he'd been a junkie for years, never quite finding a rehab program that took and often hanging in the company of other musicians—including the MC5's Wayne Kramer and Thin Lizzy's Phil Lynott and Sex Pistols Steve Jones and Paul Cook (for the Thunders' solo album *So Alone*)—who shared his habits.

So when the New Orleans coroner ruled that a drug overdose killed Thunders not long after he'd moved to the Crescent City, supposedly to record an acoustic, roots-oriented album, few raised an eyebrow.

But questions about what actually happened have lingered over the years, with friends and family believing that some manner of foul play, or at least ill intent, was involved.

Thunders—who was born John Genzale Jr. in the Queens borough of New York City—wound up in New Orleans after some circuitous travels following his departure from the Dolls in 1975.

He formed his own band, the Heartbreakers, with Dolls drummer Jerry Nolan, Television bassist Richard Hell, and Demos guitarist Walter Lure. Thunders led various versions of the Heartbreakers through 1990 while also playing in Gang War (with Kramer), the Living Dead, and the Oddballs, as well as recording six solo albums. His final studio session was with German punk band Die Toten Hosen on a version of Thunders' song "Born to Lose" just thirty-six hours before his death.

Thunders onstage with the Heartbreakers, 1977.
Erica Echenberg/Redferns/
Getty Images

Fellow musician Willy DeVille, who was living in New Orleans at the time and helped clean out Thunders' room (No. 37) at St. Peter's, offered his own guess about what happened in Legs McNeil's and Gillian McCain's book, *Please Kill Me: The Uncensored History of Punk*. DeVille said he was told by a staffer at the flophouse that Thunders had gone across the street to a club called the Pound Sterling and met up with "these two guys hanging around the French Quarter, real scum . . . selling acid." Thunders did not do LSD, but DeVille guessed that "Johnny said something like, 'Look, if you get me some cocaine, I'll put you in a hotel room there. . . .'" According to photographer Bob Gruen, Thunders was carrying at least $10,000 in cash with him shortly before leaving New York for New Orleans.

DeVille continued, "I think they crushed a tab [of LSD] and Johnny, thinking that it was blow, just went in the bathroom and hit it. All of a sudden it's LSD, and he must have been bouncing off the walls like crazy . . . . I think they dosed him and Johnny took the methadone to come down. And I think that he took so much methadone, that's what killed him." DeVille said he found two methadone boxes in Thunders' room, "and that's enough to kill the entire French Quarter."

The late Dee Dee Ramone (née Douglas Colvin) told a similar story in his memoir, *Poison Heart: Surviving the Ramones*, writing that Stevie

MYTH TRACK

Chinese Rocks," a frank paean to heroin addiction, was written by Dee Dee Ramone and Richard Hell, the latter of whom briefly played bass in Thunders' post–New York Dolls outfit, the Heartbreakers. It was the opening track on 1977's *L.A.M.F.*, the Heartbreakers' only studio album, and the fourth track on the Ramone's 1980 LP, *End of the Century*. Played by either band, it suits the nihilistic nature of Thunders' life and the inevitability of his demise.

Klasson, who played with Thunders in the Oddballs, told him "that Johnny had gotten mixed up with some bastards . . . who ripped him off for his methadone supply. They had given him LSD and then murdered him."

Nina Antonia, who wrote the authorized Thunders biography *Johnny Thunders: In Cold Blood* in 1987, as well as *The New York Dolls: Too Much Too Soon* in 2005, has noted that the amount of drugs found in the rocker's system that night was not fatal, while in *Rock Bottom: Dark Moments in Music Babylon*, Thunders' sister Marion confirmed to groupie-turned-author Pamela Des Barres that the autopsy found indications of advanced leukemia, which certainly would have weakened Thunders' tolerance for drugs.

In 1994, Thunders' manager Mick Webster told Britain's *Melody Maker* that he and the family had asked the New Orleans police to reopen the investigation, without success. "They haven't been particularly friendly," Webster said. "They seemed to think this was just another junkie who had wandered into town and died. They simply weren't interested," even though, Webster maintains, parts of the police report were missing.

The original 1991 rulings, then, stand as the official explanation for Thunders' death, and likely will remain that way. He's survived by four children—three sons and a daughter—from his one and only marriage. "The whole thing is just sad," said Dolls' frontman David Johansen. "Johnny Thunders was an immensely talented man and . . . a great rock 'n' roll character. It's all just . . . tragic." ✖

CHAPTER 15

WHO KILLED KURT COBAIN?

DID POST–PUNK POSTER BOY KILL HIMSELF AS WAS REPORTED— OR WAS IT REALLY ABOUT A GIRL?

O n April 8, 1994, Nirvana frontman Kurt Cobain was found in the spare room above the garage (a.k.a. "the greenhouse") of his Seattle home, dead from a self-inflicted shotgun wound to the head.

The gun lay across his body, and a suicide note was found nearby.

At least that's the official story. And there seems little reason to doubt it. In his final days, weeks, and months, Cobain was on a downward spiral that seemingly was destined to end just as it did. His heroin addiction and additional drug intake had escalated, and while on tour in Europe just a month earlier, he'd attempted suicide in a Rome hotel with an overdose of the tranquilizer Rohypnol.

At the same time, his personal relationships were coming asunder. He turned down a lucrative deal for Nirvana to headline the Lollapalooza tour, effectively breaking up the band. He became estranged from friends and from his management team, whom he intended to fire. And, allegedly, he intended to divorce his wife, Courtney Love, as their relationship became increasingly toxic.

Cobain had his assistant, Dylan Carlson, purchase a shotgun—a Remington Model 11—ostensibly "for protection and because of prowlers." Carlson, apparently, was oblivious to his boss' recent suicide attempt and rationalized the purchase. "I don't think he was planning to kill himself," he told interviewer Nick Broomfield in the 1998 film *Kurt & Courtney*. "If he

Kurt Cobain in a Dutch studio, just as Nirvana's popularity exploded. *Michel Linssen/Redferns/ Getty Images*

had been suicidal from the outset, he would have used the gun that day."

After a painful intervention attended by Love, Cobain's managers and label representatives, Nirvana tour guitarist Pat Smear, his daughter Frances' nanny, and a counselor, Cobain finally agreed to get treatment, but not before suffering another near-fatal overdose that he toughed out in the backseat of his car.

Cobain entered the Exodus Recovery Center in Marina Del Rey, California, only to exit two days later, hopping over the facility's back fence, as legend has it. He bought himself a plane ticket back to Seattle, after which there were several sightings of him in the city.

Love, still in L.A. doing press for Hole's album *Live Through This*, frantically worked the phones trying to locate her husband. She even hired a private detective, Tom Grant, via an ad in the Yellow Pages (more on him later). Over the next few days, Cobain and Love's house was searched several times, including by Grant, but to no avail. None of the parties had ventured into the greenhouse, however.

That is the place, it turned out, that Cobain had gone, taking with him a long letter he'd inscribed "To Boddah," an imaginary childhood friend in which he talked about his overall disillusionment with life and music, quoting Neil Young's infamous line that "it's better to burn out than to fade away." He also carried towels, a quantity of Mexican black tar heroin large enough to be fatal to most users, a can of Barq's root beer, and the shotgun. Police say he cooked and injected the heroin, put the shotgun barrel into his mouth, and pulled the trigger.

His body was discovered by Gary Smith, an electrician hired to install security lighting, who saw Cobain's body lying on the floor of the greenhouse. The date of Cobain's death was estimated to be three days prior, April 5, and its cause ruled a suicide.

Most have accepted that verdict. Cobain, after all, had tried suicide before, was deeply addicted to drugs, suffered from depression and bipolar disorder, and had unstable interpersonal relationships with nearly everyone he was in contact with. He also suffered from chronic stomach pain, which was his rationale for abusing heroin in the first place. He also had "suicide genes," as two of his uncles had killed themselves—using guns, no less.

But a cottage industry has grown up around Cobain's death, and various individuals have claimed that he was murdered. Chief among them is Grant, the private detective hired by Love to find Cobain after he'd bolted from rehab. Grant contends that Cobain's credit card was used after the time of his death, suggesting foul play. He also argues that the level of heroin in Cobain's system was too great for anyone to successfully fire a gun. Grant charges that the police work surrounding the case was shoddy and that there were no fingerprints found on the shotgun, raising the possibility that the perpetrator had wiped the gun clean. And, he says, Cobain's letter

As his life came asunder, Cobain became estranged from friends and colleagues. *KMazur/ WireImage/Getty Images*

was not a suicide note, but rather an announcement of his withdrawal from the band and his impending divorce from Love. Only the last few lines suggest that he was about to commit suicide, and they could have been added by the murderer, according to Grant.

Additional claims by Grant include that the Rome incident was not a suicide attempt on Cobain's part and that Cobain's attorney, Rosemary Carroll, was instructed to draw up a new will that excluded Love because of his plans to divorce her. *That*, Grant ultimately charges, was the motivation for the murder.

Some, but not all, of Grant's theories have been debunked in one fashion or another, and he maintains a website about the matter: cobaincase.com. Other parties, meanwhile, have entered the fray. Among them are journalists Ian Halperin and Max Wallace, who have written two books on the topic, both with Grant's cooperation: 1999's *Who Killed Kurt Cobain?* and 2004's *Love and Death: The Murder of Kurt Cobain*. Hank Harrison, Courtney Love's estranged father, is solidly behind the murder theory, and has written his own book, *Kurt Cobain: Beyond Nirvana*.

Most of the Kurt-was-murdered principals appear in Broomfield's film, as do a host of other characters of questionable repute, including Eldon "El Duce" Hoke, a punk singer who claims Courtney Love offered him $50,000 to "whack" Cobain. He passed a polygraph test on the matter, but was himself murdered in 1997. Broomfield's investigation into the matter led him to say that he does not believe in any of the conspiracy theories.

Some of Cobain's musician friends are not so sure, however. In 2005, Sonic Youth's Kim Gordon told *Uncut* magazine that she believed Cobain was murdered. Her then-husband and band mate, Thurston Moore, however, speaks for a lot of Cobain's friends, fans, and followers when he says he doesn't know for sure, but something about his death strikes a false note.

"Kurt died in a very harsh way," Moore said. "It wasn't just an OD. He actually killed himself violently. It was so aggressive, and he wasn't an aggressive person; he was a smart person, he had an interesting intellect. So it kind of made sense because it was like: wow, what a fucking gesture. But at the same time it was like: something's wrong with that gesture. It doesn't really lie with what we know." ✖

DID KURT COBAIN WRITE HOLE'S *LIVE THROUGH THIS* ALBUM?

JUST FOUR DAYS AFTER COBAIN WAS FOUND DEAD of a self-inflicted gun-shot wound, his wife, Courtney Love, and her band, Hole, released what turned out to be their ironically titled second album, *Live Through This*. The album never charted well but eventually sold more than two million copies world-wide and was a critical breakthrough, receiving almost universal acclaim.

But how much of the album's combination of raw emotion and pop smarts was Love's labor and how much—if any—was due to input from Cobain?

"All this time, I have never addressed this," she told *The Observer* in 1998. "But here I am finally saying for the very first time that Kurt did not [write] *Live Through This*. I mean for fuck's sake, his skills were much better than mine at the time—the songs would have been much better. That's the first thing."

Perhaps, but that didn't stop tongues from wagging about the fact that the songs were, well, good—something Hole's sloppy punk rock had never really been. Wouldn't it seem logical that Cobain, who'd taken punk rock to the mainstream with Nirvana's *Nevermind*, could do it again with his wife's album?

Loosing Love on the general populace would seem to be Cobain's idea of a good joke. But it would be a joke at Love's expense, not exactly a gallant thing for a husband to do. And while some of the song lyrics and/or concepts— "Doll Parts," for example—seem in line with Cobain's interests, and some do follow the soft verse/loud chorus format familiar to Nirvana listeners, the songs don't really sound like the rest of Nirvana's output.

Love wasn't above asking Cobain for help here and there, though. He did sing backup on a couple songs on *Live Through This*, including "Asking for It." More damning, perhaps, was the discovery that Hole once lifted a Nirvana track (at least in part) without credit (at least initially). Seattle newspaper *The Stranger* revealed that "Old Age," appearing as the B-side of Hole's "Beautiful Son" single (and credited to Hole), was actually a Nirvana outtake from the *Nevermind* sessions with new lyrics by Love. The original can be heard on the Nirvana's *With the Lights Out* box set.

As for the authorship of *Live Through This*, only one other person besides Love knows for sure, and he's not talking.

ALL AGES SHOW.....

FROM SEATTLE, WASHINGTON

SUB POP RECORDS

NIRVANA

27 DEVILS
JOKING
& SPECIAL GUESTS
MONKEY
SHINES
$5 AT THE DOOR
TUESDAY JUNE 27TH 7PM-11PM
AT ROCKIN T.P. SANTA FE

MONKEY SHINES

BRIAN'S CARLEY

MYTH TRACK

Recorded during Nirvana's final studio session, "You Know You're Right" speaks to both Cobain's perpetual inner torment and his often wry way of expressing it. "Things have never been so swell," he deadpans in the song's chorus, before adding "I have never failed to feel/ Pain," punching the last word with a scream that seemingly emanates from the core of his being. It was the last song the band ever finished and appeared on the 2002 compilation simply titled *Nirvana*.

For many fans and friends, Cobain's death strikes a false note. *Charles J. Peterson/Time & Life Pictures/Getty Images*

CHAPTER 16

HAVE YOU SEEN THIS MAN?

FOR SOME ARTISTS, DEATH ISN'T THE END, BUT MERELY A CAREER MOVE.

ELVIS PRESLEY

The King, 1975.
*Fotos International/
Getty Images*

If Elvis Presley were alive today, you'd have to think we'd have found out by now. But wait—you mean he *isn't* alive? "The King is gone" may be the party line taken by most sentient beings, but true believers look past Presley's untimely death at the age of forty-two and will him back to life, reporting Elvis sightings from all over: the King of Rock 'n' Roll at the Burger King, perhaps, or maybe at the movies (not onscreen, mind you, but in line, buying a ticket like everyone else). Or maybe that's him at a dive bar in the South somewhere, fronting a fierce little rockabilly band and imitating his former self. As singer Mojo Nixon has pointed out, "Elvis is everywhere." Presley has become a *tabula rasa*, a blank slate upon which America—and indeed, the entire world—can project anything imaginable, be it matters of politics, pop culture, or even religion. "No one, I think, could have predicted the ubiquity, the playfulness, the perversity, the terror, and the fun of this, of Elvis Presley's second life," wrote critic Greil Marcus in his book, *Dead Elvis*. Maybe Elvis is sitting somewhere and having a laugh at our expense—watching it all on a big flat-screen TV, a Glock by his side just in case. But we doubt it.

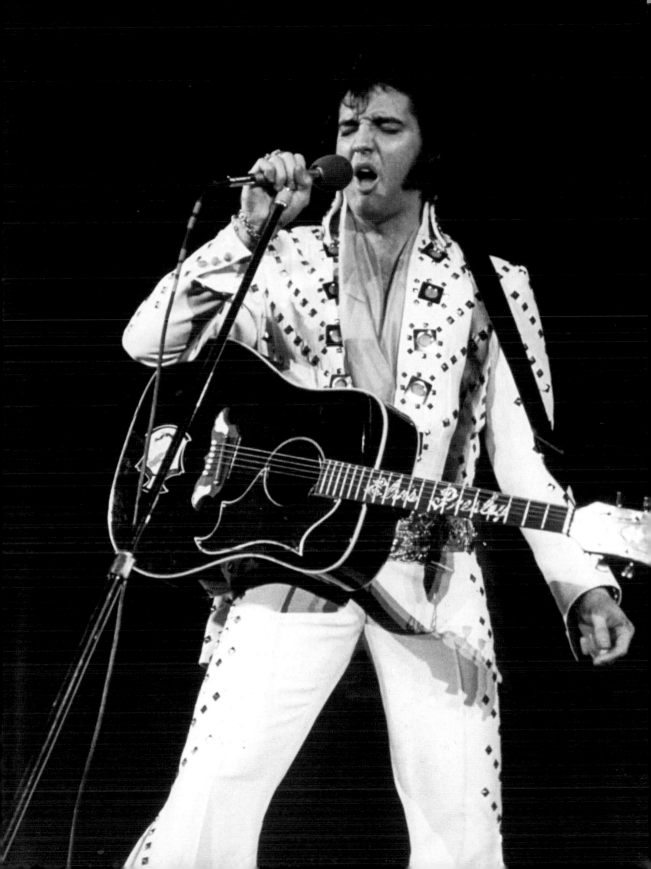

Jim Morrison, 1967.
*Michael Ochs Archives/
Getty Images*

JIM MORRISON

Unlike Elvis, Doors frontman Jim Morrison has not been sighted anywhere since July 3, 1971, when he (reportedly) died in his Paris apartment at the mythical age of twenty-seven. The story at the time was that his girlfriend, Pamela Courson, found him in the bathtub, already gone from what were termed "natural causes." There was no autopsy because there was no evidence of foul play, and when Doors manager Bill Siddons traveled to Paris—with keyboardist Ray Manzarek asking him to make sure Morrison was indeed dead—he was greeted by a sealed coffin and a death certificate. Various causes for his death have been cited over the years, most revolving around a drug overdose, most likely heroin. The uncertainty helped fuel suspicions that perhaps Morrison faked his death to escape the spotlight he found oppressive, and in the first editions of their Morrison biography *No One Here Gets Out Alive*, Jerry Hopkins and former Doors office staffer Danny Sugerman wrote that the idea is "not as far-fetched as it might seem" and that "not only is it exactly the sort of prank Jim would pull . . . but with Pamela's devoted help, could actually, incredibly, pull it off."

Courson died in 1974 without having said anything other than that Morrison was, indeed, dead. In later versions of the book, Hopkins and Sugerman recanted the theory, though acknowledging that "there remained and probably always will be those who refuse to believe that Jim is dead and those who will not allow him to rest in peace." That's certainly been the case at Paris' famed Père Lachaise Cemetery, where Morrison's grave resides alongside those of many famous European artists, heavily graffitied and regularly visited by fans leaving messages just in case Morrison came by to pick them up. Punk rocker Stiv Bators of the Dead Boys had his ashes sprinkled there after his death in 1990.

TUPAC SHAKUR

Tupac Shakur was gunned down in Las Vegas on September 7, 1996, and died six days later of respiratory failure and cardiac arrest. Or so it's said by people who accept things like . . . physical evidence. The belief that Pac is still alive stems largely from the seemingly endless flow of new music from the rapper. His posthumous output far outstrips the handful of albums he released while he was still vertical. The unsolved mystery of his murder has lent credence to the legend as well. Some accounts pinned the crime on rival rapper Notorious B.I.G., who vehemently denied the accusations right up until his own mysterious murder. Others blamed members of the Crips, with whom Shakur and Death Row label chief Suge Knight tussled earlier that evening. Still others say Knight—who was wounded in the hail of bullets—was actually behind the shooting.

Tupac Shakur, 1994.
Ron Galella/WireImage/
Getty Images

Yet, it's the idea that Tupac is still alive—that he's escaped to a tropical island somewhere, or is simply lying low waiting for the right time to resurface—that continues to intrigue fans. Never mind that even a cursory listen to Pac's recent output yields little more than the sound of the repeated scraping of the bottom of the barrel. The inherent contradictions in Tupac's life and career, it seems, make him too enticing a figure to let go. As writer Danyel Smith has pointed out, "Tupac keeps you searching, even now for the line between how one rolls through life and how one rocks the microphone. Crazy motherfucker. Coward. Sucker. Sexist. Sex symbol. Provocateur. Hero." ✗

CHAPTER 17

DID JOHN LENNON AND BRIAN EPSTEIN REALLY . . . YOU KNOW . . . ?

WEEKEND IN SPAIN—TRUE TRYST OR MERE TITILLATION?

Brian Epstein loved his men—that would be the Beatles, whom he managed from 1962 until his death from a drug overdose in 1967. And Epstein loved men, as a discreet but fairly open (in his circles) homosexual.

The question is, did he love one of the Beatles, specifically John Lennon, in that way, and was it ever reciprocated?

It's a story that has circulated through Beatles lore for decades. Epstein's homosexuality in general (which was illegal in Britain at the time) and fancy for Lennon, in particular, were common knowledge in the group's camp. Ray Coleman, among the most reputable of Lennon's many biographers, termed it a "fixation" in his book, *Lennon: The Definitive Biography*, and wrote that Lennon was well aware of it. Longtime Epstein and Beatles associate Peter Brown wrote in *The Love You Make: An Insider's Story of the Beatles* (with Steven Gaines) that Epstein "was dazzled by John, by his looks, by his wit, even his cruelty" and lived in "the eternal hope that one day [Epstein] might consummate the relationship."

Whether Epstein did just that during a four-day vacation he and Lennon took to Barcelona, Spain, in late April 1963—just three weeks after the birth of Lennon's first son, Julian—became the basis for one of the most enduring rumors surrounding the Beatles. It was this trip that generated gossip that an affair actually happened and created a bit of a cottage industry of

speculation over copulation, as well as analysis and argument. It also led to some awkward and even violent moments around the closely guarded interior of the Beatles' world.

Three varying, and conflicting, accounts have been attributed to Lennon himself. In 1980, he told *Playboy* interviewer David Scheff that his relationship with Epstein "was almost a love affair, but not quite. It was never consummated. But it was a pretty intense relationship. It was my first experience with a homosexual that I was conscious was homosexual." In Spain, Lennon said, he and Epstein "used to sit in cafés and Brian would look at all the boys and I would ask, 'Do you like that one, do you like this one?' I was rather enjoying the experience, thinking like a writer all the time: I am experiencing this, you know. It was just the combination of our closeness and the trip that started the rumors."

In the famous "Lennon Remembers" interview with *Rolling Stone* founder Jann Wenner, Lennon called himself "a bastard" for leaving his wife and newborn son to go to Spain and acknowledged that, "I watched Brian picking up the boys. I like playing a bit faggy, all that. It was enjoyable, but there were big rumours in Liverpool, it was terrible. Very embarrassing."

I'M A

BEATLES

BOOSTER

Pete Shotton, a friend of Lennon's since childhood in Liverpool and a member of his pre-Beatles band the Quarrymen, related a much more graphic description of the trip in his book, *John Lennon: In My Life*. Shotton claimed Lennon told him that during the vacation, "Eppy just kept on and on at me, until one night, I finally just pulled me trousers down and said to him: 'Oh, for Christ's sake, Brian, here, just stick it up me fucking arse, then.' And he said to me, 'Actually, John, I don't do that kind of thing. That's not what I like to do.' 'Well,' I said, 'what is it you like to do?' And he said, 'I'd really just like to touch you, John.' And so I let him toss me off, and that was it. . . . Yeah, so fucking what! The poor bastard. He's having a fucking hard time anyway. So what harm did it do, then, Pete, for fuck's sake? No harm at all. The poor fucking bastard, he can't help the way he is."

Epstein himself never made any public comment on the rumors about Spain. But in his book *Lennon Revealed*, Larry Kane—who covered the group's 1965 American tour—wrote that Epstein had made a pass at him one night over dinner in his room at the Beverly Hills Hotel. Kane gently deflected the overture but asked Epstein the following night in San Diego about the trip to Spain. "He responded, 'Larry, I love John, but nothing (pause) nothing happened.' It was simply an impossibility."

Other Lennon biographers have offered their own interpretations of the trip. May Pang, Lennon's mistress during an estrangement with second wife Yoko Ono, maintained that "the likelihood of John having an affair with Brian Epstein is absurd, and actually impossible." Coleman wrote, "As one who was close to [Lennon] during the Beatles' rise to fame, I saw a solidly heterosexual man. He did not boast about his exploits, but he made it abundantly clear that he enjoyed women. John would hardly have taunted Brian so mercilessly about his sexual preferences if he felt an empathy with him as a homosexual."

In *The Love You Make*, however, Brown and Gaines contended that Lennon grudgingly allowed Epstein to have his way with him: " . . . back in their hotel suite, drunk and sleepy from the sweet Spanish wine, Brian and John undressed in silence. 'It's okay, Eppy,' John said, and lay down on his bed. Brian would have liked to have hugged him, but he was afraid. Instead, John lay there, tentative and still, and Brian fulfilled the fantasies he was so sure would bring him contentment, only to awake the next morning as hollow as before."

Albert Goldman, in his reviled *The Lives of John Lennon*, not only wrote that Epstein and Lennon did have sex, but that they "did not confine themselves to a single sexual experiment in Spain. They were sexually involved for the balance of Brian's life. . . ." But, Goldman posited, the relationship was about control on Lennon's part, specifically understanding the control he exerted over Epstein because of the latter's attraction. Goldman wrote that Lennon explained to subsequent Beatles manager Allen Klein, "I had to control the man who had control over our lives and our careers." And Paul McCartney, though he's firmly dismissed any notion of a Lennon-Epstein affair over the years, did feel that Lennon had ulterior and manipulative motives in going to Spain with Epstein. "John was a smart cookie," McCartney noted in an interview with London's Capital Radio. "Brian was gay, and John saw his opportunity to impress upon Mr. Epstein, who was the boss of the group. I think that's why he went on holiday with Brian. And good luck to him, too—he was that kind of guy; he wanted Brian to know whom he should listen to. That was the relationship. . . . So they say he went on holiday with someone who was known to be gay and therefore he is gay."

The alleged Lennon-Epstein affair was also the subject of *The Hours and Times*, a 1991 feature film directed and written by Christopher Munch that dramatized the trip to Spain but trod lightly on any sexual encounters.

One thing's for sure: Lennon was not happy with the rumors about him and Epstein when they returned from Spain. He was disarmed by questions from female staffers at Epstein's office in Liverpool. And during McCartney's twenty-first birthday party on June 18, 1963, a drunken Lennon assaulted and seriously injured Bob Wooler, a local disc jockey and longtime Beatles supporter, for allegedly calling him "queer." In some accounts, Wooler asked Lennon, "How was the honeymoon?"—meaning his trip with wife Cynthia rather than the vacation with Epstein. The incident necessitated a public apology by Lennon. ✕

MYTH TRACK

During the early '80s, openly gay British rocker Tom Robinson posited a theory that the Beatles song "You've Got to Hide Your Love Away," which appears on the 1965 *Help!* soundtrack, was about Epstein's closeted homosexuality. Lennon acknowledged that the song was part of his "Dylan period," but never discussed its lyrical inspirations.

CHAPTER 18

WERE THOSE REALLY SHARKS THAT LED ZEPPELIN CAUGHT IN SEATTLE?

THE MUD SHARK'S ROLE HAS BEEN GREATLY EXAGGERATED IN THIS FISH TALE.

Rock 'n' roll history does not lack for stories about sex, groupies, kinky diversions, lurid hotel room encounters, and even bestiality. The most notorious of these wrapped all of them together: Led Zeppelin's infamous "Shark Episode."

It's actually a true story, of course—the servicing of a groupie with a saltwater craniate, at least—but a number of untruths developed around the tale over the years. There was, for instance, no shark.

The event occurred during July 1969, when Led Zep was on tour with Vanilla Fudge and both bands played at the Seattle Pop Festival. The groups were staying at the Edgewater Inn, a four-story facility on Puget Sound where guests can famously cast a line into the water and catch fish from their hotel rooms. The lobby gift shop even sold rods, reels, and bait.

Zep drummer John Bonham and tour manager Richard Cole had had a particularly good night, reeling in a large quantity of mud sharks and red snappers into the wee hours and stowing them in a wastebasket filled with water. After boasting of their success the next day, the pair had a number of visitors to Bonham's second-story room, including some particularly adventurous groupies. Cole wrote in his memoir, *Stairway to Heaven: Led Zeppelin Uncensored*, that Jackie, a seventeen-year-old redhead from Portland, stood out from the pack: "[She] was one of the few birds I had ever met who could drink us under the table. She was chugging champagne

Led Zeppelin in 1969. Perhaps pondering the finer points of ichthyology. *Michael Ochs Archives/ Getty Images*

Just a couple of guys hanging out, talking about fishin'. Robert Plant and Zep manager Richard Cole, 1973. *Express Newspapers/ Getty Images*

from the bottle, talking openly about sex, spicing up her sentences with salty language. And she seemed to be trying to bait us into doing something daring."

Jackie's desire was bondage, and the Zep and Fudge entourage was willing. After tying her naked to the bed with a length of rope, Cole took one of the red snappers and placed it into Jackie's nether regions—apparently much to her pleasure. "It was pretty disgusting . . . pretty nutso," recalled Fudge drummer Carmine Appice. "It was just another crazy night on the road."

Cole wrote, "The whole incident was something that I just wanted to do and that I had never done before. Perhaps it was a cheap thrill. I knew we would get away with it simply because we had gotten away with most things. . . . Jackie certainly never complained. . . . At one point she asked me not to stop." The ministrations ended after about a half hour, when Cole became "bored with the whole thing."

Adding to the legend was the fact that the Fudge's Mark Stein filmed the incident, with various musicians and hangers-on taking turns posing in the frame with the ecstatic groupie. Appice said the raw film was subsequently purchased by Randy Pratt, one of the Fudge's financial backers, but there's some question as to whether it's ever been developed or shown. Upon hearing about the encounter, Frank Zappa wrote a song, "The Mud Shark," which became a concert favorite and appeared on the Mothers' live album, *Fillmore East—June 1971*.

Cole, meanwhile, noted that the "Shark Episode" quickly took on a life of its own: "Rumors circulated that the girl had been raped . . . that she had been crying hysterically . . . that she had pleaded for me to stop . . . that she had struggled to escape . . . that a shark had been used to penetrate her. None of the stories was true."

The "Shark Episode," Cole noted, did, however, become "a metaphor for the worst of rock music's personal vandalism . . . the definitive example of the 'debauchery' and 'depravity' running rampant through the rock music world. And Led Zeppelin was cast as the worst of the lot."

Cole and Bonham, in fact, tried a similar "experiment" with a groupie and a Great Dane at Los Angeles' Chateau Marmont, but it was the beast rather than the beauty that wasn't interested in that particular brand of whole lotta love. ✖

MYTH TRACK

Time and again, Frank Zappa turned to tales of encounters between rock musicians and groupies as fodder for his songs. One of these became "The Mud Shark," a track from the Zappa/ Mothers album *Live Fillmore East—June 1971*. In it, Zappa recounts the tale, as it was told to Mothers keyboardist Don Preston by members of the Vanilla Fudge during "a chance meeting at the Chicago O'Hare airport." Zappa describes the hotel, and how you can rent fishing gear and fish from your window, but rather than lay out the details of the actual sex act performed on a "succulent young lady . . . with a taste for the bizarre," he instead creates a dance called the Mud Shark that he says is "sweeping the ocean." Curiously, Led Zeppelin is never mentioned in the song.

CHAPTER 19

DID JOHN PAUL JONES MISTAKE A TRANSVESTITE FOR A FEMALE GROUPIE?

WHAT A DRAG . . . ZEP BASSIST BRINGS A "WOMAN" BACK TO HIS HOTEL ROOM AND EVENING GOES TO POT.

Ask almost any groupie, especially a veteran of the hedonistic '70s, and they'll tell you the most notorious, predatory, and insatiable band on the rock 'n' roll road was Led Zeppelin. The British group's exploits are legendary and comprise a veritable lexicon of rock debauchery.

Of course, those tales generally involve women—except for one.

During a stop in New Orleans on the group's 1973 tour, bassist/keyboardist John Paul Jones reportedly found himself in a compromising position with a man—who was dressed as a woman. The encounter took place at the Royal Orleans hotel and supposedly inspired the song "Royal Orleans" on Led Zep's 1976 album, *Presence*.

In his book, *Stairway to Heaven: Led Zeppelin Uncensored*, the group's longtime road manager Richard Cole wrote that "a couple of drag queens" were flirting with Jones in the hotel bar, "as if they had found their 'catch' for the evening." One, known as Stephanie, wound up in Jones' room, where the couple fired up a joint. Apparently they fell asleep in bed while smoking, igniting a fire and setting off alarms. A city fire crew, axes and hoses in hand, put out the blaze.

Cole adds that Jones contended "that he hadn't known the transvestite was a man. He looked sincere during his explanation, but no matter what the truth really was, we knew we had caught him in a rather embarrassing

It's always the quiet guy, isn't it? John Paul Jones performs with Led Zeppelin, circa 1972. *Michael Putland/Getty Images*

situation. 'We're not going to let Jonesy forget about this one for a long time,' I told Robert [Plant]."

It is, in fact, one of the few wild Zep stories about Jones, who was the most reserved and quiet member of the group, and frustrated his band mates by keeping his own counsel and even disappearing for periods of time.

Jones has not denied that he and Stephanie wound up in a room together, or that he fell asleep and set the room on fire. But he told *Mojo* magazine that Cole got some of the finer points wrong. "That I mistook a transvestite for a girl is rubbish; that happened in another country, to somebody else," he said. "The truth is much more prosaic than the myth, but what annoys me is Cole's story makes me look like a fool."

Jones, in fact, says there's no love lost between him and Cole after the former road manager served as a major source for Stephen Davis' revealing *Hammer of the Gods: The Led Zeppelin Saga* before penning his own *Stairway to Heaven*. "I've never spoken to him again," Jones said.

And Jones, by the way, will not give up the identity of the "somebody else" who *did* mistake a transvestite for a woman in another country. ✖

MYTH TRACK

"Living Loving Maid (She's Just a Woman)" appeared on the *Led Zeppelin II* album well before Jones' supposed encounter with the drag queen, but it certainly presaged some of the sentiments he might have felt at the time.

20

DID MICK JAGGER AND DAVID BOWIE SPEND THE NIGHT TOGETHER?

ZIGGY STARDUST AND JUMPING JACK FLASH TOGETHER IN BED? MOST LIKELY MAKING LOVE TO THEIR EGOS . . .

One is Ziggy Stardust, Aladdin Sane, Major Tom, and the Thin White Duke. The other is Jumping Jack Flash and the Midnight Rambler—and you can call him Lucifer.

Any way you look at it, that's a lot of folks to get into one bed. But when David Bowie and Mick Jagger were revealed to be sleepover buddies—by Bowie's ex-wife, no less—gossip mongers surely got more than a little bit of satisfaction, although exactly what happened under the covers between the two British rockers remains something of a mystery.

As singers and showmen, Jagger and Bowie are cut from the same cloth—similar influences, similar flamboyance, similar interest in playing with perceptions of sexuality. They share many of the same early rock and R&B influences, and Bowie, who's younger by three and a half years, certainly lists Jagger as a source for his gender-bending persona and lithesome stage moves. However, Bowie has been outspoken and proud about his bisexuality, whereas Jagger has always maintained a lady killer reputation, certainly before and even during his marriage to Bianca De Macias.

Cut from the same cloth. David Bowie and Mick Jagger, 1985. *Ron Galella/ WireImage/Getty Images*

Not surprisingly, the two became fast friends—and friendly rivals—reportedly meeting backstage after a Bowie concert during the spring of 1973. They were documented hanging out at nightclubs, attending concerts, sitting ringside at the second Muhammad Ali–Ken Norton fight in 1973, and chatting it up at Bowie's first "retirement" party at the Cafe Royal

Bowie and Jagger in London in 1999, six years after Angela Bowie's accusations. *Denis O'Regan/Getty Images*

in London. Bowie, according to Jagger biographer Christopher Andersen, began introducing his friend to gay culture, including films.

Ava Cherry, one of Bowie's backup singers, contended that "Mick and David were really sexually obsessed with each other. Even though I was in bed with them many times, I ended up just watching them have sex. They became very close and practically lived together for several months." Leee Black Childers, a onetime employee at Bowie manager Tony Defries' MainMan firm, added that "everyone knew what was going on between them."

The big reveal, however, came on May 4, 1990. That's when Angela Bowie, who divorced the singer in 1980 and was celebrating the expiration of a ten-year gag order that was part of the settlement, appeared on *The Joan Rivers Show* and announced that she had once walked in on her husband and Jagger. "I caught him in bed with men several times," Angela told Rivers and her other guest that day, radio shock jock Howard Stern.

"In fact the best time I caught him in bed was with Mick Jagger"—naked, she added.

In her subsequent memoir, 1993's *Backstage Passes*, Angela—who's one of many rumored subjects of the Rolling Stones' 1973 hit "Angie" (which Jagger has denied)—wrote that the *coitus interruptus* took place during the fall of 1973 at the Bowies' Oakley Street home in London. She had just returned from a trip to New York and was told by the maid, "I think Mick and David are asleep upstairs." Angela headed to the bedroom, "and there indeed they were, asleep in our bed. I asked them if they wanted coffee, and they said yes. And that was that."

Well, there was more . . .

"There are two ways of looking at the incident," Angela wrote, noting that it could have been "best friends" sleeping off a night of hard partying. "I really don't like the automatic assumption that if two men are found in bed together, something sexual must be happening. . . . On the other hand, however, I think the assumption was correct. Or to put it another way, when I walked into that room and found Mick and David together, I felt absolutely dead certain that they'd be screwing. It was so obvious, in fact, that I never even considered the possibility that they *hadn't* been screwing. . . . I didn't have to look around for open jars of K-Y Jelly." ✗

The Bowie-Jagger rumblings further fueled another longstanding Stones rumor—that the Stones' 1973 hit "Angie" was about Angela Bowie.

MYTH TRACK

Jagger and Bowie covered not a little of the same musical ground (Bowie's "Rebel, Rebel" may be the best Rolling Stones song the band never wrote), but the place to hear them together is their 1985 rendition of Martha & the Vandellas' Motown smash "Dancing in the Streets," which the two recorded for the 1985 Live Aid concerts and subsequently released as a single.

WAS DONNA SUMMER SELF-LOVIN' IN THE STUDIO?

DISCO QUEEN TURNS STUDIO ORGASMS INTO HER FIRST HIT. YES, SHE WAS FAKING IT.

With "Love to Love You Baby," Donna Summer came on the music scene in a big way in 1975. But she didn't come in quite the manner that was purported at the time.

Word on the street, and in the clubs, was that the song's ecstatic cooing was the sound of Summer having an orgasm—or more—in the recording session. *Time* magazine even reported that Summer achieved twenty-two orgasms during the sessions with producers Pete Bellotte and Giorgio Moroder.

Turns out Summer was a pretty convincing actress. "I didn't need a lot of words," Summer recalled, "so I oohed and aahed my way through it. I was imagining if Marilyn Monroe sang the song, that's what she would do."

She did claim, however, to perform the vocal while lying on the floor so she wouldn't have to look at the production team behind the control room glass. "I wasn't going to sing like that with four guys looking right at me," Summer said. "I was a little too modest for that, even with that kind of song."

The irony is that Summer was an unlikely candidate to record that kind of song at all, never mind the vocal embellishments. Born LaDonna Gaines in Boston, she was a trained gospel singer raised by devout Christian parents before she left home to take a part in a German production of *Hair*, followed by stints in *Godspell* and *Show Boat*. Returning to the United

Both hands where we can see them, please. A pensive Donna Summer, circa 1975. *Fotos International/ Getty Images*

States in 1971, she began recording under her given name, changing it when she married Austrian actor Helmuth Sommer (switching the spelling, of course, to Summer), whom she divorced in 1976.

Summer began singing backup at recording sessions in New York, where she met Moroder and Bellotte. They got her a deal in the Netherlands where she had success with a single called "The Hostage." But when Summer presented Moroder with an idea for a new song, things blew up in a big way.

"That was a song I wasn't planning on singing myself," Summer explained. "It was kind of a work in progress, and I thought that if I could get the right singer, it could be a hit. I had given Giorgio the idea of 'Love to Love You Baby,' and he went into the studio and put a track to the idea and I went in and sang some words over it."

The producers convinced Summer to record the single herself, and she never looked back. "Love to Love You Baby" reached No. 2 on the Billboard Hot 100 and No. 1 on the Hot Dance Club Play chart, though some radio stations banned it. And Summer remembers "scary" reactions to the song when she performed it live. "There'd be riots in the theaters," she said, "real riots, people fighting and trying to body slam themselves onto the stage, trying to get to me, throwing all kinds of things on stage. It just got to the point where I could not do that song."

"Love to Love You Baby" was certified gold and was the first shot in a career in which Summer has sold more than 100 million albums, won five Grammy Awards, and was even nominated for the Rock and Roll Hall of Fame.

Summer's long-term success had to do in large part with her ability to move beyond the sex-bomb image of her first hit. "I don't think I set out in any way, shape, or form to be a sexy person," she contended. "I think I set out to be an intelligent woman and to have a certain type of respectability. So when this whole thing hit, I just had to act out a part. It was like being on stage. But at some point that role got really tiring, and I decided 'I have to change this. I'm gonna have to bring some humor to this and infiltrate my real person into this creation, 'cause it isn't working for me anymore.'" ✗

The Queen of Disco works on her oohs and ahhs. *Michael Ochs Archives/ Getty Images*

All these years later, "Love to Love You Baby" remains a steamy concoction of Eurodisco propulsion and soft-porn suggestion. We recommend listening in close proximity to a cold shower.

MYTH TRACK

22

DOES STING HOLD THE SECRET TO MARATHON SEX?

EIGHT HOURS AT A TIME, IT'S BEEN SAID. KIND OF MAKES EVERY BREATH HE TAKES COUNT, NO?

Was it as good for Sting as it was for the bass? London, 1990. *Jim Steele/Redferns/ Getty Images*

In the spring of 1993, it seemed like there wasn't anything Sting couldn't do. The man once known as Gordon Sumner had been the frontman of the Police, one of the top bands on the planet, and had gone on to a successful solo career. He played rock, pop, R&B, jazz, and world music. He'd acted in films (*Quadrophenia, Dune, Brimstone and Treacle, Julia and Julia*, and more) and in a Broadway production of *The Threepenny Opera*. He started a record label (Pangea) and was an outspoken human rights and environmental activist. He was a man of wealth, taste, and great accomplishment, with residences around the globe.

So why wouldn't we believe he was capable of having sex for eight hours at a time?

It was in 1993 that Sting, a noted devotee of yoga, was speaking to Britain's *Q* magazine with his friend Bob Geldof—former frontman of the Boomtown Rats and organizer of Band Aid's "Do They Know It's Christmas?" and the Live Aid concerts—sitting in. "Geldof, a very old friend of mine, and I were in our cups one day—bullshitting, as you'd say—and forgot about the journalist sitting in the corner," Sting recalled. The conversation, according to *Q*, went something like this:

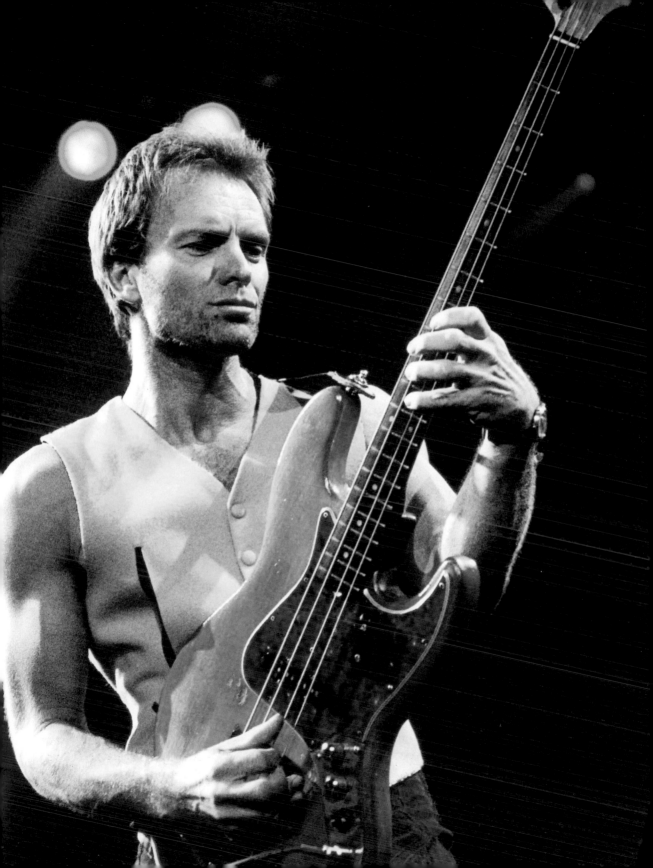

Geldof: What about that yoga thing? You're into that. Does it work?
Sting: It can take you to higher levels, yeah. I've started to use it in sex now where you don't spill your seed, you don't come. You retain it all and go on for longer. You stay erect and your stomach goes as near to the spine as you can make it while still allowing you to breathe and you never lose control, you just keep going.
Geldof: Where's the fucking fun in that? Why don't you just come? I like to come as quickly as possible. Ten seconds is about my max.

Needless to say, when the word of that exchange hit the streets, Sting's tantric sex life was hotter than Roxanne's red light. "That story flew around the world faster than anything I ever said," Sting remembered shortly afterward. "It was hilarious. I thought it was a lot of fun—it *is* a lot of fun! Actually, I'm modifying that now; it's seven hours now, not five. It depends on where you have dinner, but let's not get into that . . ."

Sting did have his fun with the rumor over the years. Though he admitted to many it was "a joke" or "a gross embellishment," he told the *London Evening Standard*, "I'm definitely not going to deny it, or confirm it. Yes, I do a lot of yoga. I'm not an expert on Tantra, but it's about trying to establish everyday normal things like walking, eating and making love with an element of the sacred." His tongue was more firmly in cheek during a BBC1 interview in 2004, when he told host Jeremy Vine, "I have frantic sex, which is just as good as tantric sex."

Some of those close to the star were less amused. Trudie Styler, Sting's companion since the early '80s and wife since 1992 (and mother of their four children), noted that, "I think [Sting and Geldof] were actually getting blotto. Sting and I have been doing yoga for so many years and I think what he was saying was that there is a lot of intimacy missed out by people having sex. But I think the lagers were being downed. The next thing I knew he was embellishing and he'd said I did tantric shopping and that I'd go shopping for five hours and then not buy anything. I told him that wasn't funny—'Just stick to your original story and leave me out of it.'" She did, however, once put Sting up for a charity auction to explain—rather than demonstrate—tantric sex to the high bidder.

Daughter Coco Sumner, meanwhile, told Britain's *Love* magazine in 2009, "It's embarrassing when people bring it up. I don't really have anything to do with my parents' sex life. They love each other. So what?" She too, however, blamed Geldof for goading her father into telling tales out of school.

If Sting was contrite about his loose lips at home, it wasn't evident in 2011 when he let out a few more details about his sex life with Trudie to Britain's *Guardian*: "I don't think pedestrian sex is very interesting. I like the theatre of sex. I like to look good. I like her to dress up. I like to dress her up. . . . Romantic? We like tawdry." Trudie, who was also part of the interview, simply noted, "We don't get bored. Being apart juices the relationship."

And if Sting isn't careful with what he says in the future, there may be a lot more juicing going on. ✗

Yoga enthusiasts Trudie Styler and Sting enjoy the Grammys, 1992. *Robin Platzer/Twin Images/Time & Life Pictures/Getty Images*

MYTH TRACK

When he recorded his first solo album, *The Dream of the Blue Turtles*, in 1985, Sting included a track called "Love Is the Seventh Wave." Given the tantric revelation that was coming, it's nice to know he was keeping track.

CHAPTER 23

WAS CIARA EVER "LIKE A BOY"?

THIS MYTH HAS LEGS . . . BUT NOTHING BETWEEN THEM.

Ciara Princess Harris—that's just Ciara to you—broke onto the scene in 2004 with her multiplatinum album *Goodies* and a pair of arresting No. 1 hits: the teasing title track, in which she shuts down a prospective lover by declaring, "You won't get no nookie or the cookies/I'm no rookie," and "1, 2 Step."

Proclaimed "First Lady of Crunk & B" by Lil Jon, who produced the "Goodies" track, Ciara saw her career continue to skyrocket with a number of collaborations, including a Grammy-winning video, "Lose Control," with Missy Elliott.

But while Ciara has been comfortable courting controversy in recent years—including beefs played out on Twitter with Rihanna and 50 Cent—that certainly wasn't the case in 2005, when Internet rumors that began surfacing wondered just what kind of "goodies" the singer might be packing.

Among the tales being told were that Ciara is a lesbian; was born a male and underwent a sex-change operation; is still male and a transvestite; is a hermaphrodite; and went on *The Oprah Winfrey Show* to admit that one or the other of the rumors is true.

Allhiphop.com "Rumors" columnist Illseed took on the controversy in 2005. "We consistently get rumors saying that Ciara, the Crunk-N-B Queen, was born with male and female genitalia," he wrote. "We have no CLUE where this crazy rumor started, but it's not true as far as we know. We're thinking that she was in the club throwin' bows a little too hard and some dude decided to start this one. Or maybe it's those mean faces, but to our knowledge, she only has one female private place. Unfortunately, I'll never see it. The rumor has good legs though and it's not dying anytime soon."

Ciara brings the goodies. New Jersey, 2011. *Michael Stewart/ WireImage/Getty Images*

That's hardly definitive, and it didn't quell the rumors, the most elaborate of which was circulated as an email purporting to include an article written by Nolan Strong, a scribe from the same site. In it, Ciara reportedly admitted that she was a lesbian on the BET program *106 and Park*.

Needless to say, that never happened, and Allhiphop.com took pains to declare the emailed article a fake, posting this on the site: "If you happen to read that AHH's own Nolan Strong wrote a story about Ciara being a trannie he/she, don't believe it. We didn't write it, but somebody is trying to be creative with starting rumors. Ciara is alllllll woman, baby!"

Again, less than definitive. But it's easy to see that such rumors can be debilitating for an artist's career, especially—and it must be said—in the hip-hop community, where virulent homophobia often goes unchecked (which is not to say that doesn't happen in other genres as well).

Still, Ciara scored a second No. 1 album with her 2006 effort, "The Evolution," on which she may have unintentionally pushed the rumor forward with the single "Like a Boy," on which she declared, "Wish we could switch up the roles." The song's video, meanwhile, showed Ciara as a tattooed, cross-dressing, crotch-grabbing playa. Appearances aside, the song and the video are just putdowns of bad male behavior.

More recently, Ciara's albums *Fantasy Ride* (2009) and *Basic Instinct* (2010) have produced hits, but her career cooled sufficiently enough that she parted with her longtime label, LaFace, and left Jive Records after only one release and signed with Epic Records.

Ciara doesn't seem to have gone out of her way to address the rumors, and over the years she's been linked romantically to rappers Bow Wow, Ludacris, and 50 Cent, as well as basketball star Amare Stoudamire. At the height of the trans/whatever controversy, however, she did say this to the *New York Daily News'* Rush and Molloy: "You know what's funny? The rumor that I used to be a man. They said Oprah said that on her show. I've never been on Oprah in my life—we all know I have years before I go on Oprah, so come on!" **✗**

The First Lady of Crunk & B attends a pre-Grammy gala in 2011. *Helga Esteb/ Shutterstock.com*

MYTH TRACK

Like a Boy," a track from Ciara's sophomore set, *The Evolution*, isn't one of the singer's biggest hits, but it's a song that comments incisively about flipping the script in terms of gender roles. But rather than listen to the song, check out the striking black-and-white video in which Ciara sports tattoos, a wife-beater, and a bad attitude.

LADY GAGA WAS BORN WHAT WAY?

POP STAR PART MAN? BET YOU CAN'T SAY THAT WITH A POKER FACE.

It's hard to be surprised by anything in the world of pop divas. Cher, Madonna, Britney, Christina, Beyoncé, Katy . . . they've all managed to cause a mythical sensation with something or other during their multiplatinum careers.

But reports that Lady Gaga is a hermaphrodite—which, she told Britain's *Q* magazine, was "the most humorous rumor of my life so far"—may have topped them all.

Gaga, born Stefani Joanne Angelina Germanotta in New York City, was still on the rise—so to speak—in 2008, but titters based on live performance photos and footage pinpointed a small bulge in her pants. Then a December 14, 2008, posting on the Starr Trash gossip blog quoted the singer and performance artist as admitting to having both male and female sexual organs: "It's not something that I'm ashamed of, [it] just isn't something that I go around telling everyone. Yes. I have both male and female genitalia, but I consider myself a female. It's just a little bit of a penis and really doesn't interfere much with my life. . . . It's not like we all go around talking about our vags. I think this is a great opportunity to make other multiple-gendered people feel more comfortable with their bodies. I'm sexy, I'm hot. I have both a poon and a peener. Big fucking deal."

While not necessarily accepted as gospel truth, the comment certainly got tongues wagging—and put a photographic bull's eye on Gaga's nether regions, resulting in more hermaphroditic "evidence." Meanwhile, Gaga further fueled the fire when she told *Rolling Stone* in its 2009 Hot Issue that she considers herself bisexual, which "intimidated" her boyfriends. She also told *USA Today*, "I don't think being gay or being bisexual or being sexually free is anything that should be hidden. Everybody has a right to

Few ever doubted Lady Gaga has cojones. The metaphorical kind, that is. *vipflash/Shutterstock.com*

Backstage at MTV's studios in Times Square. *Scott Gries/Getty Images*

their secrecy, of course, but I don't feel particularly shy about it. It is who I am. I sing very openly about it in my music, so I suppose I could say that I choose not to hide it in interviews because I don't care to hide it and, two, because it is very obvious in my music that I like women."

Being bisexual and being a hermaphrodite are two different things, however. Gaga's manager, Troy Carter, told ABC News in August 2009 that the rumor "is completely ridiculous," but his client was more coy about it. She told Australia's Fox FM radio that the subject was "too lowbrow for me to even discuss" and that "my little vagina is very offended" by the subject.

In December 2009, however, she addressed it head-on with ABC interviewer Barbara Walters, who had named Gaga one of the most fascinating people of the year. She told Walters pointedly that she is not "part man and part woman," but that the rumor didn't bother her. "At first it was very strange and everyone sort of said, 'That's really quite a story!'" Gaga told Walters. "But in a sense, I portray myself in a very androgynous way, and I love androgyny . . . I like pushing boundaries."

She displayed a sense of humor about it, at least. During a photo shoot for *Q* in early 2010, she told the crew that "I want to wear a dick strapped to my vagina," referring to using a dildo in order to make fun of the hermaphrodite story. "We all know one of the biggest talking points of the year was that I have a dick," Gaga said, "so why not give them what they want? I want to comment on that in an artistic way."

The real truth, of course, is that Gaga has laughed all the way to the bank with this one. The woman who had the cojones (metaphorical, of course) to title her first album *The Fame* before she was, well, famous, sold a combined 50 million copies worldwide, in combination with its expanded follow-up, *The Fame Monster*. She also moved a combined 51 million copies of singles such as "Just Dance" and "Poker Face," won five Grammy Awards, was *Billboard* magazine's Artist of the Year for 2010, and won a place on the *Time* 100 list of influential people. She's also the first celebrity to attract more than 10 million Twitter followers, on top of 34 million Facebook friends.

Gaga's second album, *Born This Way*, debuted at No. 1 in ten countries and moved more than 1.1 million copies in its first week in the United States—the best-selling debut since 50 Cent's *The Massacre* in 2005. The title track and first single, which many tagged as an homage to (if not an outright copy of) Madonna's "Express Yourself," was the fastest-selling single in iTunes history, moving a million copies in just five days.

"I'm very hard on myself. The pressure is more personal than anything," Gaga said before the *Born This Way* album release. "The overarching theme and concept of the record is that I'm a woman in a moment of journey that is eternal. It's sort of a journey through my psychology and how the fame has affected my life. More importantly, I wanted to sort of refute the idea of being a trend and start to procure my legacy as a musician."

And, of course, as a mythological personality. ✖

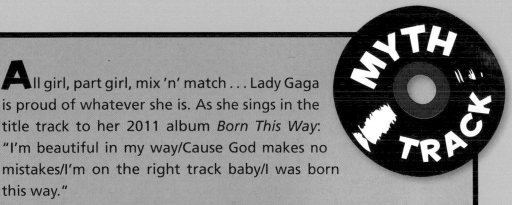

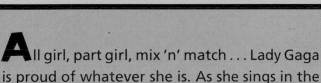

All girl, part girl, mix 'n' match . . . Lady Gaga is proud of whatever she is. As she sings in the title track to her 2011 album *Born This Way*: "I'm beautiful in my way/Cause God makes no mistakes/I'm on the right track baby/I was born this way."

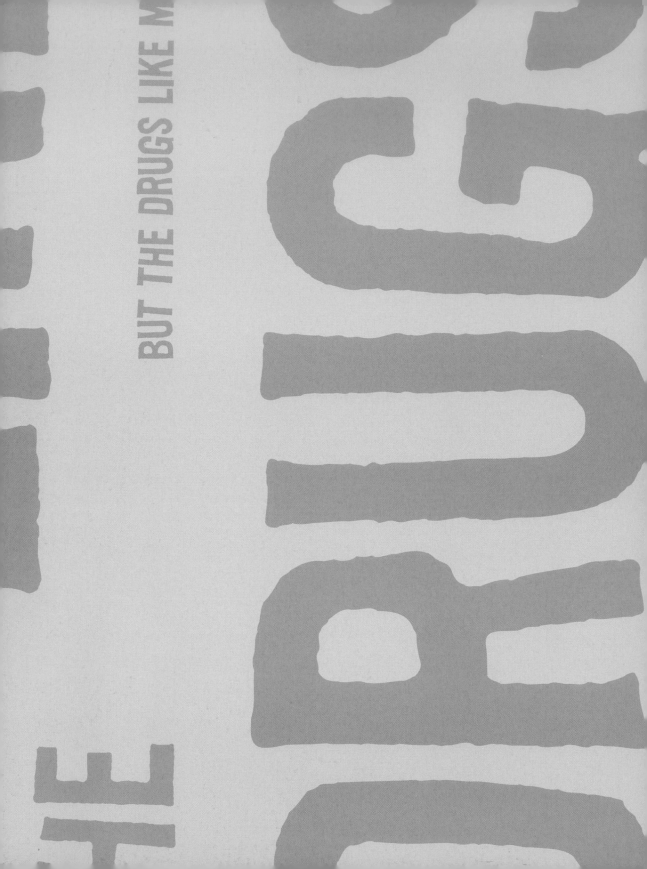

I DON'T

LIKE

THE

DRUGS

BUT THE DRUGS LIKE ME

CHAPTER 25

WAS "PUFF, THE MAGIC DRAGON" ONE TOKE OVER THE LINE?

SINGALONG CLASSIC IS ABOUT POT? YOU MUST BE STONED!

A song about a boy, a dragon, and their adventures. It's obviously about marijuana, too, right?

That's the story of "Puff, the Magic Dragon."

Written by Peter Yarrow of Peter, Paul & Mary from a poem by Cornell University classmate Leonard Lipton, "Puff" became a folk and pop classic—as well as a No. 2 hit on the Billboard Hot 100—when the trio released it in early 1963 as part of its album, *Moving*. It also became a campfire ballad and a veritable standard covered by the likes of Bing Crosby, John Denver, Marlene Dietrich, Roger Whittaker, the Irish Rover, and Alvin & the Chipmunks—not exactly a cadre of dope fiends.

So where did the myth come from? It began with a kind of underground word-of-mouth from (a) conservatives willing to believe the worst about a populist and politically left-leaning, pacifistic folk trio, and (b) countercul-turalists who thought it was pretty hip that the song was about dope (see also "Lucy in the Sky with Diamonds"). When *Newsweek* magazine cited "Puff" in a mid-'60s article about drug references in popular music, the claims received a wider and more credible airing.

The very title of "Puff," myth proponents contend, is a not-so-veiled reference to smoking, while dragon really means "draggin'," as in "on a joint." The dragon's human pal is named Jackie Paper, i.e. rolling papers. And Puff lives in the land of Honalee, a purposeful misspelling of the pot-

Peter, Paul, and Mary backstage. 1962. "You can wreck anything with idiotic analysis," Peter Yarrow observed. *Michael Ochs Archives/Getty Images*

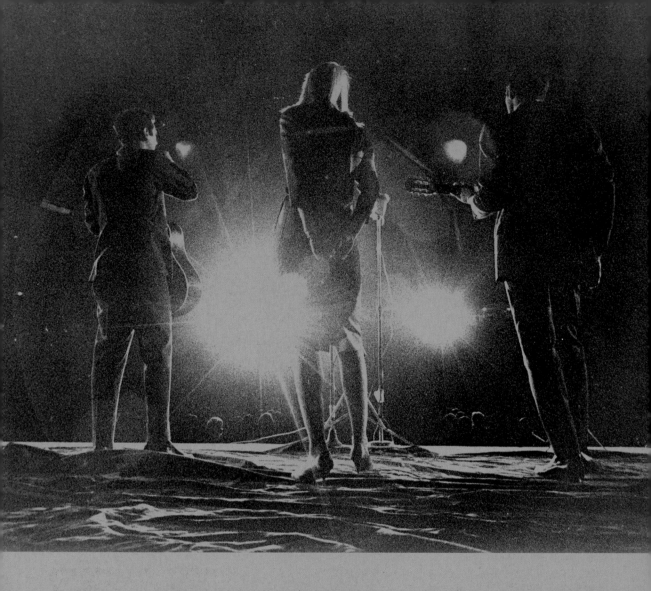

Peter, Paul, and Mary under
the bright lights, circa 1963.
Michael Ochs Archives/
Getty Images

rich Hawaiian town of Hanalei. The evidence was stacked—but not at all accurate, according to Yarrow.

"That's probably the grossest misinterpretation of a song I've encountered in my career," he says. "It came out of this witch hunt mentality of the times, where there had to be something wrong with anything that was considered lefty or counterculture. It was just . . . asinine."

His band mate, Noel Paul Stookey, recalls, "We'd always get people asking us about the drug references in 'Puff,' and you'd never know if they were angry about it or thought it was cool. It was comical at times . . . but also a shame because it detracted, I felt, from a very special and magical song."

Yarrow explains that the song and the poem are "about growing up and losing innocence, obviously." Lipton was a friend of one of Yarrow's house-mates at Cornell and was feeling homesick one evening in 1959 when he decided to vent his emotions in poetry. Inspired by the Ogden Nash piece "Custard the Dragon," he tapped out "Puff" on Yarrow's typewriter but left the poem at the house, where Yarrow discovered it. Lipton had forgotten about the poem and was working as a camp counselor when a mutual friend called to tell him Yarrow was looking for him in order to give Lipton proper credit.

Peter, Paul & Mary performed "Puff" for at least a year before recording it. For the song itself Yarrow had dropped one verse that was part of Lipton's poem; as the original sheet of paper containing the poem was lost, there's no record of it, and both Yarrow and Lipton have said they have no memory of what the verse said.

As the marijuana myth grew around it, the trio would poke fun at the misunderstanding; the trio, and Yarrow, as a solo act, would even sing a version of "The Star Spangled Banner" that they would interrupt to point out how specific lyrics could be interpreted as being about drugs (e.g., "broad stripes" refer to prison uniforms and "bright stars" allude to narcs' badges). "You can wreck anything with that kind of idiotic analysis," Yarrow would tell audiences.

And during a recorded solo performance at the Sydney Opera House in March 1976, Stookey put "Puff" on "trial," a lengthy shtick that included testimony from Puff and Jackie Paper and asked the audience to serve as the jury. Not surprisingly, "Puff" was found not guilty of drug references.

The myth persists, however. In the 2000 film *Meet the Parents*, characters played by stars Ben Stiller and Robert DeNiro engage in a furious debate about the song's true meaning. ✕

MYTH TRACK

Scores of artists of all nationalities, ages, and musical genres have recorded "Puff, the Magic Dragon" over the years. Peter, Paul & Mary's is still the definitive version (particularly the extended treatment on the 1964 *In Concert* album), but if it's trippy you're after, check out Alvin & the Chipmunks doing it on the 1965 *The Chipmunks Sing with the Children* album.

DID THE BEATLES GET STONED AT BUCKINGHAM PALACE?

I'M A
BEATLE FAN
In Case of EMERGENCY
CALL PAUL
OR RINGO

WHEN RECEIVING A HIGH HONOR, WHAT'S MORE APPROPRIATE THAN, WELL, BEING HIGH?

On October 16, 1965, when the Beatles were made members of the Most Excellent Order of the British Empire (MBE), the Fab Four were suffering both a bad case of nerves in anticipation of meeting Queen Elizabeth and mixed feelings about accepting the honor at all.

Given to both military and civilian recipients, the MBE comes with nominal benefits. In *The Beatles Anthology*, Paul McCartney says he was told it came with a stipend of "£40 a year, and you get to go into St. Paul's Whispering Gallery for nothing." In other words, aside from the spiffy silver medal—which McCartney and George Harrison later wore on their *Sgt. Pepper* jackets—hardly worth the trouble of showing up to collect it.

Worse was the potential impact on the Beatles' image. As emerging pop icons and counterculture heroes, an alignment of any sort with the British Empire could be seen as—and indeed, might even be—exactly the wrong move.

"We had to do a lot of selling out then," John Lennon later groused. "Taking the MBE was a sellout for me."

On another level, though, Lennon fiercely argued that the band deserved it, perhaps more than certain other recipients. "Lots of people who complained about us getting the MBE received theirs for heroism in the war," he said. "Ours were civil awards. They got them for killing people. We deserve ours for not killing people."

Lennon was also bowled over by the actual ceremony. "Although we don't believe in the Royal Family, you can't help being impressed when you're in the palace, when you know you're standing in front of the Queen," he said. "It was like a dream."

And then the moment came. "To start with, we wanted to laugh," Lennon recalled. "But when it happens to you, when you are being decorated, you don't laugh anymore. We, however, were giggling like crazy because we had just smoked a joint in the loos of Buckingham Palace, we were so nervous. We had nothing to say. The Queen was planted on a big thing. She said something like, 'ooh, ah, blah, blah' we didn't quite understand. She's much nicer than she is in the photos."

Or as McCartney would later put it, "Her Majesty's a pretty nice girl, but she hasn't got a lot to say."

The fact that even John Lennon could be intimidated by such a scene seems somewhat unlikely, since he was the Beatle who, during a 1963 command performance before the Queen, instructed the audience, "Would the people in the cheaper seats, clap your hands. And the rest of you, if you'd just rattle your jewelry."

The Beatles mug with their MBEs at Buckingham, 1965.
Rolls Press/Popperfoto/ Getty Images

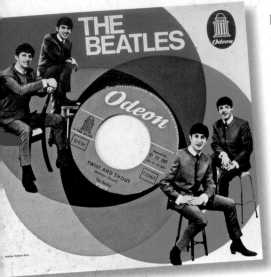

Still, the notion of a group of rock 'n' rollers being typical bad boys and nipping off for a quick joint before the ceremony is completely plausible. There's only one problem: It didn't happen.

"We never smoked marijuana at the investiture," George Harrison said, completely deflating the myth. "What happened was we were waiting to go through, standing in an enormous line with hundreds of people, and we were so nervous that we went to the toilet. And in there we smoked a cigarette—we were all smokers in those days.

"Years later, I'm sure John was thinking back and remembering, 'Oh, yes, we went in the toilet and smoked,' and it turned into a reefer. Because what could be the worst thing you could do before you meet the Queen? Smoke a reefer! But we never did."

In the end, of course, McCartney was made a Knight of the Realm in 1997. He had no qualms about accepting the accolade at that late date, but later grumbled it allowed him to "get a good table at restaurants without reservations. Sometimes." As for Lennon, he returned his MBE in 1969, "in protest against Britain's involvement in the Nigeria-Biafra thing, against our support of America in Vietnam and against 'Cold Turkey' [his solo single] slipping down the charts." No telling if any mind-altering substances were involved in the composition of that postcard. ✗

MYTH TRACK

Even if the Beatles didn't indulge at their MBE ceremony at Buckingham Palace, marijuana became both a hobby and an inspiration for the Fab Four, especially McCartney. His song "Got to Get You into My Life" is not about a girl, but is rather a paean to pot, "like someone else might write an ode to chocolate or a good claret," McCartney said in Barry Miles' book, *Many Years from Now*. "It wouldn't be the first time in history someone's done it, but in my case it was the first flush of pot."

SO, WHO TURNED ON THE BEATLES IN THE FIRST PLACE?

IT'S OFTEN BEEN SAID THAT NONE OTHER THAN BOB DYLAN introduced the Beatles to marijuana, a notion that McCartney has confirmed on at least one occasion.

The Beatles were aware of the drug, McCartney claimed, but hadn't tried it. "I mean, we'd heard all the jokes: that the Ray Charles band had been at the Hammersmith Odeon and the cleaner said, 'He must be really tight, that Ray Charles—there are two of his musicians sharing a ciggy in the toilet.' We thought it was funny, but it wasn't us. Then Bob came round to our hotel, and he said to us, 'Here, try a bit of this.'"

Once again, it's Harrison who busts the balloon. "We first got marijuana from an older drummer with another group in Liverpool," he said. "We didn't actually try it until after we'd been to Hamburg. I remember we smoked it in the band room in a gig in Southport. . . . Everybody was saying, 'This stuff isn't doing anything.' It was like that old joke where a party is going on and two hippies are up floating on the ceiling, and one is saying to the other, 'This stuff doesn't work, man.'"

Still, it may be Dylan who got the band properly high for the first time, with the bonus buzz generated by getting to hang with one of their heroes. And even that meeting was the result of a misunderstanding, at least according to Lennon. "Dylan had heard one of our records where we said, 'I can't hide,' and he had understood, 'I get high,'" Lennon reported. "He came running and said to us, 'Right, guys, I've got some really good grass.' How could you not dig a bloke like that?"

Bobbies attempt to restrain Beatles fans outside of Buckingham. *Ted West & Roger Jackson/Central Press/Getty Images*

CHAPTER 27

DID GEORGE JONES REALLY DRIVE HIS LAWNMOWER TO THE LIQUOR STORE?

APPARENTLY, YES. BUT FORGET ABOUT ALL THOSE OTHER OLD EX-WIVES' TALES.

After a long day of lawn care, "The Possum" finds some shade. *Michael Ochs Archives/Getty Images*

George Jones' voice earned him the sobriquet "the greatest living country singer." But his penchant for drink and drugs caused him to blow off shows in bunches and made him even more famous as "No Show Jones."

"I've retained many lawyers, and one told me that I had been sued more than a thousand times in my career, mostly for failing to honor personal-appearance contracts, because I was too drunk, or too full of drugs, or both, to do the shows," Jones wrote in his 1996 autobiography, *I Lived to Tell It All*.

Jones' dissolute ways led to all manner of mayhem: He trashed hotel rooms, picked fights with men twice his size, fired a gun at a friend (thankfully, he missed), and shot holes in the floor of his tour bus. Once, when he believed his then-wife Tammy Wynette was having an affair with country star Porter Wagoner, he followed Wagoner into a restroom and found him standing at a urinal.

"I walked up behind him and shouted, 'I want to see what Tammy's so proud of!'" Jones recalled. "Then I reached around and grabbed his dick. I twisted hard."

You'd think that little episode would pretty much top everything in Jones' arsenal of drunk tales. But no. In the mid-1960s, when he was married to his second wife, Shirley Ann Corley, Jones took a ride to the liquor store that assured his notoriety for a boundless thirst would go hand in hand with his fame as a singer. Jones wrote of the incident:

Once, when I had been drunk for several days, Shirley decided she would make it physically impossible for me to buy liquor. I lived about

eight miles from Beaumont [Texas] and the nearest liquor store. She knew I wouldn't walk that far to get booze, so she hid the keys to every car we owned and left.

But she forgot about the lawn mower.

I can vaguely remember my anger at not being able to find keys to anything that moved and looking longingly out a window at a light that shone over our property. There, gleaming in the glow, was that ten-horsepower rotary engine under a seat. A key glistening in the ignition.

I imagine the top speed for that old mower was five miles per hour. It might have taken an hour and a half or more for me to get to the liquor store, but get there I did.

Jones did it again in the 1970s, when he was married to Wynette—or so she claimed in her 1979 autobiography, *Stand By Your Man*.

"I got into the car and drove to the nearest bar 10 miles away," Wynette wrote. "When I pulled into the parking lot there sat our rider-mower right by the entrance. He'd driven that mower right down a main highway. He looked up and saw me and said, 'Well, fellas, here she is now. My little wife, I told you she'd come after me.'"

It's possible that Wynette's story was fabricated, however. Her book is filled with stories that Jones vociferously denies, including one in which Jones broke the heels off of a closetful of her shoes so she couldn't run away from him and another far more damning one in which he shot a gun at her.

Fact or fiction, Jones has made the most of his reputation. He turned the lawnmower story into his 1996 single, "Honky Tonk Song," and the video embellished the tale even further to include a police chase. Jones has also appeared in other artists' videos—including Hank Williams Jr.'s "All My Rowdy Friends Are Coming Over Tonight" and Vince Gill's "One More Last Chance"—each time entering the scene atop a riding mower.

With the help of his fourth wife, Nancy Sepulvedo, whom he married in 1983, Jones has jettisoned his more destructive vices, including drinking, drugging, and smoking. "They can have all the drink they want right on the same table, and it doesn't bother me whatsoever," he said in a 2009 interview. "And I can't stand the smell of cigarettes. I smoked 'em for fifty-some years. I quit smoking and drinking, all at the same time."

He has occasionally backslid, however. In 1999, Jones suffered a near-fatal car accident that was fueled by vodka. But he swore off again, claiming the crash "put the fear of God in me." That time, it should be noted, he was driving a Lexus, not a John Deere. ✖

Tammy looks on in 1973 as George is fitted by famed Hollywood tailor Nudie Cohen. *Michael Ochs Archives/Getty Images*

There's no shortage of George Jones songs celebrating alcohol and making light of the mischief that he's gotten himself into because of it. However, "If Drinkin' Don't Kill Me (Her Memory Will)," a No. 8 country hit for Jones in 1981, is anything but a good-time tale of excess. Instead, the song gives a sense of the ruin that alcohol has wrought in Jones' life, both in his relationships and on his health.

CHAPTER 28

DID HENDRIX PUT LSD IN HIS HEADBAND?

**JIMI'S ALLEGEDLY ACID–FILLED HEADWEAR.
WHAT A TRIP!**

Grace Slick commanded those listening to her psychedelic drug ode "White Rabbit" to "feed your head."

Some say Jimi Hendrix did just that.

A regular part of the virtuosic southpaw guitar legend's look was some form of headband, usually a scarf positioned across his forehead at the bottom of his Afro and tied in the back. And, some maintained, it was often dressed up with some LSD.

Hendrix was certainly no stranger to the drug. He and his mates in the Jimi Hendrix Experience were reportedly turned onto acid during a visit to San Francisco, though road manager Gerry Stickells later termed that first trip "grim." Nevertheless, Hendrix made LSD part of his regular drug diet, often tripping with fellow musical buddies such as Beatles Paul McCartney and John Lennon. Hendrix was subtle about it, however; Chas Chandler, Hendrix's producer and onetime roommate, commented to biographer John McDermott that "I didn't even know they were on acid. . . . I was living in the same flat as Jimi and I had no idea." Hendrix's use of the drug would eventually become a point of conflict with Chandler, particularly during the making of the *Electric Ladyland* album in 1967 and 1968.

Acid helped fire up Hendrix's performance—literally, at the Monterey Pop Festival in 1967—and many fans suspect LSD had something to do with his uniquely stylized version of "The Star Spangled Banner" made

"Ouch! The lysergic acid diethylamide is stinging my eyes!" Not. Hendrix sports his ever-present headband in 1970. *Jorgen Angel/ Redferns/Getty Images*

famous at the Woodstock Music & Art Fair two years later. The drug also became a bonding agent between Hendrix and manager Michael Jeffrey, again much to Chandler's chagrin.

Even though some reports have him soaking his headbands in liquid LSD before he'd take the stage, there is no evidence or eyewitness documentation of Hendrix ingesting LSD through the pores of his scalp (it's doubtful that this is even physiologically possible) or that he ingested LSD-laced sweat that streamed down his face to his mouth. Others maintain he taped as many as fifty hits onto the inside of a scarf. (Another rumor says that Hendrix took heroin through the tip of his penis, but we'd rather not go there.) Billy Cox, Hendrix's latter-day bassist, once said that the acid-in-the-headband stories were "bull, just plain stupid. Yeah, people were taking [acid], but not like that. That's one of the stupidest stories I've ever heard."

In the end, the drug that brought Hendrix down was Vesparax, a sleeping pill he took upon returning from a party in the wee hours of September 18, 1970. Hendrix reportedly took nine of the powerful tablets (which combined three different drugs: brallobarbital, secobarbital, and hydroxyzine) and vomited in his sleep, ultimately suffocating himself. Murder theories have been floated over the years, but none have been taken seriously. ✗

MYTH TRACK

In the title track to the Jimi Hendrix Experience's 1967 debut album, *Are You Experienced?*, Jimi sings about "Trumpets and violins I can hear in the distance/I think they're calling our names." Maybe there was something in that headband after all.

CHAPTER 29

WAS THE BEATLES' "LUCY IN THE SKY WITH DIAMONDS" ABOUT LSD?

OR JUST A TRIPPY ACRONYM THAT JOHN LENNON SAID WAS QUITE ACCIDENTAL?

Throughout his life, John Lennon never wavered from his account of how the Beatles' "Lucy in the Sky with Diamonds" came to be. As he told *Playboy* in 1980, "My son Julian came in one day with a picture he painted about a school friend of his named Lucy. He sketched in some stars in the sky and called it *Lucy in the Sky with Diamonds*. Simple."

Well, not so simple.

When the song was released on the Fabs' landmark *Sgt. Pepper's Lonely Hearts Club Band* album in 1967, the tenor of the times being what it was, conservatives and counterculturalists alike looked at the title and thought one thing: LSD.

The perception would have serious ramifications. The BBC banned the song that year because of its acronym, as did some radio stations in the United States. Some anti-Beatles groups, still bitter over Lennon's August 1966 remark that the Beatles were more popular than Jesus, used the song as another point of attack, although there weren't wholesale burnings of *Sgt. Pepper's* as there were of other Beatles records back then. Lennon, however, maintained to *Playboy* that the LSD connection was "purely unconscious. . . . Until someone pointed it out, I never even thought of it. I mean, who would ever bother to look at the initials of a title? It's *not* an acid song."

Quoted in *The Beatles Anthology*, Lennon reiterated that "Lucy" "never was [about acid] and no one believes me. I swear to God, or swear to Mao, or to anybody you like, I had no idea it spelt LSD."

Rather, as Lennon contended to *Playboy*, "The images were from *Alice in Wonderland*. It was Alice in the boat. She is buying an egg, and it turns

Portrait of the artist as a young man. Julian and his dad in 1968. Manchester Daily Express/*SSPL* via *Getty Images*

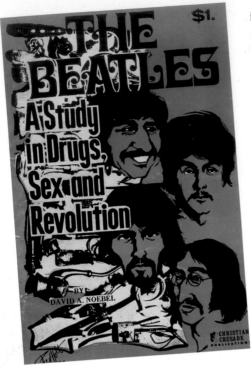

The Beatles' druggin' ways—real, perceived, or embellished—often elicited strong responses from the squares, including this 1969 tract. *Voyageur Press Collection*

into Humpty Dumpty. The woman serving in the shop turns into a sheep and the next minute they were rowing in a rowing boat somewhere, and I was visualizing that. There was also the image of the female who would someday come save me—a 'girl with kaleidoscope eyes'—who would come out of the sky. It turned out to be Yoko [Ono]. . . . So maybe it should be 'Yoko in the Sky with Diamonds.'"

Doesn't sound drug-influenced at all, does it?

Some, of course, found the LSD reference easy enough to believe because, by that time, Lennon and the Beatles were immersed in swinging London's burgeoning psychedelic drug scene. George Harrison and Lennon had been introduced to acid, which was not illegal at the time, in 1964 by someone Harrison referred to as "the wicked dentist" and quickly discovered its value for both altering and opening their minds. "The first time I had acid, a light-bulb went off in my head and I began to have realizations which were not simply, 'I think I'll do this,' or 'I think it must be because of that,'" Harrison noted in *The Beatles Anthology*. "An illumination goes on inside. . . . My brain and my consciousness and my awareness were pushed so far out that the only way I could begin to describe it is like an astronaut on the moon, or in his spaceship, looking back at the Earth. I was looking back at the Earth from my awareness."

But while the Beatles were drug proponents at the time, Lennon noted in the *Anthology* he only took LSD once in the recording studio and felt it was a mistake. For *Sgt. Pepper's*, he remembered, "We didn't really shove the LP full of pot and drugs but, I mean, there *was* an effect. We were more consciously trying to keep it out. You wouldn't say, 'I had some acid baby, so groovy,' but there *was* a feeling that something had happened between *Revolver* and *Sgt. Pepper.*"

Lennon's friend Pete Shotton was an eyewitness to Julian showing his father the "Lucy" picture, "which he described as "a pastel drawing of his classmate Lucy's face against a backdrop of exploding, multicolored stars." John, he added, was "unusually impressed with his son's handiwork"—enough to use it as the basis of a song. "Though John was certainly ingesting inordinate amounts of acid around the time he wrote 'Lucy in the Sky with Diamonds,' the pun was sheer coincidence," Shotton said.

Ringo Starr claimed he was there as well "when Julian came in with this little kid's painting, a crazy little painting, and John, as his dad, said, 'Oh, what's that?' and Julian said, 'It's Lucy in the sky with diamonds.' And then John got busy."

Julian's nursery-school classmate, by the way, was Lucy Vodden O'Donnell. "I don't know why I called it (*Lucy in the Sky with Diamonds*) or why it stood out from all my other drawings, but I obviously had an affection for Lucy at that age," Julian told *The Guardian* newspaper in 2009. "I used to show Dad everything I'd built or painted at school, and this one sparked off the idea." In 2007, O'Donnell herself told the BBC, "I remember Julian and I both doing pictures on a double-sided easel, throwing paint at each other, much to the horror of the classroom attendant. . . . Julian had painted a picture, and on that particular day his father turned up with the chauffeur to pick him up from school."

After O'Donnell died in 2009 from lupus, Julian recorded a version of "Lucy" and released it as an EP, with proceeds going to lupus research organizations. The disc includes a copy of the original drawing, which Pink Floyd's David Gilmour now owns.

The Beatles began working on "Lucy" on February 28, 1967, in Abbey Road's Studio Number Two. It was the eleventh track they recorded for *Sgt. Pepper's*. The song has been covered by Natalie Cole, the Black Crowes, Bono and The Edge of U2, Cheap Trick, and William Shatner. The most famous version, however, was by Elton John in 1974, which hit No. 1 on the Billboard charts. Lennon, who guested on the recording under the pseudonym Dr. Winston O'Boogie, joined John to perform "Lucy" live on November 28, 1974, at New York's Madison Square Garden in what would be his final public performance. ✖

MYTH TRACK

You've heard the Beatles' version of "Lucy in the Sky with Diamonds," what, a million times at least? So treat yourself to one that's even farther out there—perhaps William Shatner's take on his 1968 album, *The Transformed Man*, or the "Luci in the Sky with Demons" parody by Marilyn Manson & the Spooky Kids on the 1992 tape *The Family Jams*.

30

WHAT WERE THOSE CHAMBERS IN JERRY GARCIA'S GUITARS REALLY FOR?

DEAD LEADER KEPT SECRET STASHES INSIDE HIS AXES? GO STICK THAT ONE SOMEWHERE.

Is that a pre-amp device in your guitar, or are you just happy to see me? Jerry Garcia noodles on *Tiger*, 1972. *Michael Putland/ Getty Images*

With no judgment intended, drugs and the Grateful Dead went together like tie and dye. It's never been a secret, nor did the band ever try to hide it from the world. It just came with the territory for the vanguard band of the '60s psychedelic-rock movement.

The Dead certainly held its drugs close during its long, strange trip as a band—but in the case of late guitarist Jerry Garcia, not quite as close as some thought.

Legend long held that *Wolf* and *Tiger*, two of the five guitars custom-designed for Garcia by luthier Doug Irwin, each contained a discreet area within its body where the hirsute Dead cofounder kept his stash.

The story has been passed through the ranks of Deadheads for decades. But the idea is far more inventive—and utilitarian—than Garcia's and the guitar-maker's intent.

Thomas Lieber, who worked as an intern for Irwin during the mid-'70s, acknowledges that there were empty spaces inside each of the instruments, but it was "not really the case" that they were designed to stash drugs. On *Tiger*, he says, the cavity was used for a pre-amp device, while on *Wolf* it was just a dead part of the design alongside the circuit board and electronics. (He does note, however, that a bass for Jack Casady of Jefferson Airplane and Hot Tuna most definitely had an area for stashing drugs, at Casady's request, as well as a decorative inlay made of hashish on the twenty-fourth fret.)

Wolf, meanwhile, was distinguished by a brass cigarette holder near the tuning peg for the low E string, where Garcia could keep a cigarette. The luthier decided to add the feature after receiving the guitar for some modifications and noticing burn marks in the peghead area where Garcia previously rested his smokes.

Tiger and *Wolf* enjoyed a historic run with Garcia from the early '70s on. *Tiger*, in fact, was the last guitar he played during his final concert with the Dead: on July 9, 1995, at Chicago's Soldier Field, a month before his August 9 death from a heart attack at the Serenity Knolls rehabilitation center in Forest Knolls, California. After a legal battle, ownership of the instruments reverted to Irwin per Garcia's will (the Dead organization maintained they were band property). Irwin, in need of cash at the time, sold them at auction for a record combined $1.74 million, with the maple-bodied *Wolf* fetching $789,500 from a private collector in Utica, New York, and *Tiger* going for $957,500 to Jim Irsay, owner of the National Football League's Indianapolis Colts.

Irsay knew all about the stash box legend and says it was one of the things that drew him to the rather elaborate guitar, whose wood layers are made of cocobolo, vermilion, and maple (later referred to in guitar circles as the "hippie sandwich"). "I really wanted *Tiger*, just the way the guitar looks and that little bit of history with Jerry's stash box hidden in there somewhere, along with the J. Garcia (signature) on the fretboard. That made it the big one to me," Irsay explains. Chris McKinney, Irsay's personal guitar tech, says they went looking for the supposed area and did find "a small cavity off to the side that at that moment had a piece of foam in it. It'd be a nice spot to hide whatever you wanted to hide."

Tiger currently resides in a special case behind Irsay's desk in the Colts' offices and practice facilities. He occasionally displays it in public and even once allowed a Deadhead to play it as a birthday present. He says that the Dead's Bob Weir has asked him to consider loaning it to the band if it were to ever open a museum. "For the most part it's about sharing it with people," Irsay notes, "to let people hold it and see it and do all those sorts of things. And obviously you feel a responsibility for taking care of it and bringing it forward." ✕

Closeup of the *Wolf*'s bridge and controls. *David Le Franc/Gamma-Rapho via Getty Images*

Ridin' that train, high on cocaine. . . ." So begins "Casey Jones," the second single from the Grateful Dead's *Workingman's Dead* album in 1970, one of two albums the group would release that year (*American Beauty* followed four and a half months later) and a nod to something that Jerry Garcia could have kept inside his guitar if the stories were indeed true.

CHAPTER 31

WAS AMERICA'S "HORSE" A BUNCH OF JUNK?

"A HORSE WITH NO NAME" IS ABOUT HEROIN? OKAY, WE'RE HOOKED.

Three nice boys from U.S. military families stationed abroad and playing acoustic guitars—likely suspects for a song about heroin, right?

That was America's lot as its first single, "A Horse with No Name," galloped to No. 1 on the Billboard 100 chart and achieved platinum sales in 1972. The band also received a Grammy Award for Best New Artist. It was an auspicious career start for a trio whose members were probably candidates for Least Likely to Cause Trouble honors at London Central High School.

That's where Gerry Beckley, Dewey Bunnell, and Dan Peek met during the late 1960s. All three were born in the United States but spent their teen years in London, where their air force officer fathers were stationed. They played in two separate bands but joined forces in 1969 after Peek had made a brief trip to attend college back in the States. Focusing on songcraft and vocal harmonies, they began playing around London and eventually wound up with Warner Bros. Records, working on their debut album with producer Ian Samwell at Trident Studios.

Bunnell, who wrote "A Horse with No Name" (initially titled "Desert Song") and debuted it at the Horrogate Festival in 1971, insists that "it was definitely not about drugs. It really was about a desert, as simple as that is. Being in the air force, we traveled around a lot, and my brother and I, wherever we happened to be stationed, the one constant was going to the

Dewey Bunnell, Dan Peek, and Gerry Beckley cop a rest after galloping to platinum success. *Gems/ Redferns/Getty Images*

America hides out in a grassy field, with no horse in sight. *Gems/Redferns/ Getty Images*

woods or the desert or down to the beach or whatever environment we were in and poke around and catch lizards and do that kind of stuff."

His father was stationed for a time at Vandenberg Air Force Base near Lompoc, California, and Bunnell recalls "being really overwhelmed by the expanse of the Southwest in the U.S. and driving through and visiting my uncle in New Mexico. It's still to me an incredibly powerful place to be, to stand out there reflecting in the quiet and the sights and the sounds of the desert. That was really the motivation behind the song."

But, Bunnell acknowledges, the meaning of "A Horse with No Name" has also "morphed a little in my mind over the years. It does take on a little bit of a different sheen to me, a little bit more of a meditative quality. So while when I wrote it, the desert was a place of wonder; now it could be more of a place of sanctuary or shelter away from the hordes."

"A Horse with No Name" was not initially included on America's self-titled debut album but was appended later, and the rereleased album also hit No. 1 in the United States. Listeners were all too ready to assume that the horse in question was actually heroin ("horse" being common slang for the drug) and that Bunnell's lyrics referred to a drug trip. Singer-songwriter Randy Newman, in fact, even dubbed it a song "about a kid who thinks he's taken acid." Initially the group didn't mind the attention: "When we first came out, the two biggest things were 'Why did you name yourself America?' and 'Is this [song] about heroin?'" Bunnell recalls. "That was probably a big part of its mystique. Above and beyond the song or the melody, I think people were all intrigued—'Oh wow, man, those guys are only nineteen years old and are already heroin addicts or something. Well, give me a break. That was certainly not it. But whatever gets you to the dance is fine."

The amusement turned to alarm, however, as some radio stations used the perceived drug reference as an excuse to ban the song from their playlist. "We really had to get out there and explain it wasn't about heroin so that they'd play the next song," Bunnell recalls.

America, and Bunnell in particular, also took some heat for the song's sonic similarity to Neil Young—so much so that when it first came out, many assumed "A Horse with No Name" was, in fact, a new Young song. Young was an acknowledged influence on all three band members, and Bunnell recalls, "I was the one who took the brunt of the, 'Hey, these guys are Neil clones.' It was flattering in a way, but that's not how it was intended."

America eventually distanced itself from the comparisons, scoring three platinum and three gold albums, as well as eight Top 40 hits between 1971 and 1975. Peek left the group in 1977 and passed away in 2011, but Bunnell and Beckley have soldiered on—still, of course, playing "A Horse with No Name." And on their 2011 covers album, *Back Pages*, they nodded again to Neil Young with a rendition of Buffalo Springfield's "On the Way Home." ✖

MYTH TRACK

What, do you think we're going to recommend "Daisy Jane" or something? "A Horse with No Name" remains America's biggest hit and a standard-bearer for the California singer-songwriter sound of the early '70s—even if the group was based in England. Comedian Richard Jeni did, however, advise the group, "You're in the desert. You got nothing else to do—name the freakin' horse!"

CHAPTER 32

DID STEVIE NICKS HAVE A BUMP OF "BACKDOOR" BLOW?

FLEETWOOD MAC'S GOLD DUST WOMAN SAYS YOU CAN SHOVE THAT ONE UP YOUR BUTT.

Cocaine was part and parcel of '70s rock, and it was particularly prevalent in the California scene. If you were selling albums like Fleetwood Mac was at that time—including more than 40 million units worldwide of 1977's *Rumours*—you could certainly afford enough Peruvian marching powder to keep the troops moving around the world. Multiple times. The group's coke dealer even got an acknowledgment in the *Rumours* liner notes.

"It was all over the place, all the time," Stevie Nicks recalled. "We didn't think much about it. It was just one of those things you did, like, every day. It's pretty sick when you look back on it, but at the time it was part of your regular existence." Nicks told Jenny Boyd—sister of Pattie Boyd, George Harrison and Eric Clapton's ex-wife and author of the 1992 book *Musicians in Tune*—that cocaine helped her overcome stage fright: "You're scared to walk onstage in front of a bunch of people. . . . To get away from that you have a drink, or whatever anybody else does, and you get brave and so you don't have to experience that terrible fear. . . . Then that becomes a habit."

A certain naïveté was also part of her experience. "I absolutely remember people saying it's recreational," Nicks told *The Hartford Courant*. "It's not addictive, it's excessive. It's the rich man's drug. It's something you do once in a while and have a good time. Nobody ever said anything about that it could remove your brain from your head."

Nicks paid a greater price than many for her addiction. She has freely acknowledged that excessive cocaine use left her with a significant hole in her septum. "I have very delicate tissue," she confirmed to *Q* magazine,

Stevie Nicks said the Peruvian marching powder helped her overcome stage fright. *Fin Costello/Redferns/Getty Images*

"so it ate away my nose. It's so painful. I curse the day I ever did cocaine. Nothing really works right in my head now."

There were reports, however, that Nicks' nose did not work right enough to snort the conventional way. The alternative: having a crewmember take a straw, or some similar instrument, and blow the blow into her anally. It's become a favorite story—both backstage and in the seats—but Nicks has consistently claimed it's not at all true. "I hate when it comes up," she told *Q* in 2011. "It makes me so angry because of course it never happened and I don't understand why someone said that about me in the first place. I am such a lady and so very prudish and all about wearing lots and lots of lingerie and clothes—I'm the opposite of that story. It's just so insane and disgusting and makes me nauseous. Whoever set that story off, I hope they rot and burn in hell."

Nicks finally dealt with her drug hell in 1986. After being warned by a plastic surgeon that her cocaine habit could have long-term consequences, she checked herself into the Betty Ford Center following a Fleetwood Mac tour of Australia. As part of that process, however, a psychiatrist put her on Klonopin, a particularly strong and equally addictive tranquilizer. Nicks' dependence on *that* drug lasted nearly seven years, during which she gained considerable weight and suffered vocal deterioration.

"I was told, 'If you take this, you probably won't go back to cocaine,'" she told *US* magazine. "Finally I said OK. And in the next eight years I did so much that I regret. I fired people. I didn't care. You don't really feel much when you take this stuff. . . . You have a feeling of calmness that is so overwhelming, you have no soul left. . . . I'm pissed because I missed 10 years. I went from my thirties to my fifties. Isn't that a drag?"

Nicks finally kicked Klonopin through a forty-seven-day detox in 1993 and 1994 and has been, by all reports, drug-free ever since. ✗

MYTH TRACK

The keening, nervy "Gold Dust Woman" was the B-side to "You Make Loving Fun," the fourth single off of the mega-platinum *Rumours* album, peaking at No. 9 on the Billboard Hot 100. Dig around and you'll find cover versions by Hole, Sheryl Crow, Sister Hazel, Grace Potter & the Nocturnals, and—we kid you not—Waylon Jennings.

DID WILLIE NELSON REALLY GET BAKED AT THE WHITE HOUSE?

ON THE ROOF AGAIN . . . THE RED–HEADED STRANGER SPARKS ONE UP ABOVE THE OVAL OFFICE.

O ther than Snoop Dogg, or maybe the late Bob Marley, Willie Nelson is the go-to guy when it comes to dope-smoking musicians. And he may, in fact, be the living champion. In 2009, Snoop took to Twitter to report, "only person that every [*sic*] smoked me out is willie mothafuckn nelson!!! straight O.G."

Nelson is a longtime pot enthusiast and advocate for its legalization. "It's a matter of time, a matter of education, a matter of people finding out what cannabis, marijuana, is for, why it grows out of the ground and why it's pre-scribed as one of the greatest stress medicines on the planet," he said.

In recent times, however, Nelson has paid the price for his love of the leaf. He's been busted several times, most recently in 2010. After he posted bail for that arrest, harmonica player Mickey Raphael told the press that the bust was actually a boon to Willie's health regimen. "He lost six ounces," Raphael cracked.

Back in 1978, Nelson was in the first flower of true celebrity, having sold a million copies each of albums like *Red Headed Stranger*, *Wanted: The Outlaws*, *Waylon & Willie*, and *Stardust*. Nelson was invited to the White House by President Jimmy Carter, who was a fan and had attended his concerts while serving as governor of Georgia. Nelson played a show on the White House lawn for an event honoring NASCAR drivers that was hosted by First Lady Rosalynn Carter, who gamely joined Nelson for a duet on Ray Wylie Hubbard's "Up Against the Wall Redneck Mother."

The Red-Headed Stranger onstage with his favorite guitar, *Trigger*, in 1979. *Michael Ochs Archives/ Getty Images*

Seriously.

Carter himself, meanwhile, was not there, but was at Camp David, brokering a peace accord between Egypt's Anwar al Sadat and Israel's Menachem Begin. Nelson and his then-wife Connie were invited to sleep in the Lincoln bedroom. Before retiring, Nelson and one of Carter's sons—under the watchful eye of Secret Service agents—climbed up on the White House roof and smoked a joint.

Nelson later returned to the White House to play a show with Carter in attendance and may have even repeated his ritual on the roof. "I would guess that Willie and my sons knew a lot more about that than I did," Carter said.

Still, the president remained a fan who relaxed during stressful times by tying fishing flies in his study while Nelson's songs played on the stereo. "So all the good things I did or, of course, all the mistakes I've made, you could kind of blame half of that on Willie," he later joked. ✖

MYTH TRACK

Willie Nelson's propensity for smoking mass quantities of high-quality pot is well known, as is his ability to outsmoke just about anybody who dares to board his tour bus. Country superstar Toby Keith and fellow songwriter Scott Emerick tempted fate and somehow managed to tell the tale in a hilarious song called "I'll Never Smoke Weed with Willie Again." According to legend, that's a pledge that Jimmy Carter's sons never took.

MORE CANNABIS SHENANIGANS IN THE CARTER WHITE HOUSE

NELSON, HOWEVER, WAS NOT THE FIRST notable musician to spark one up at the White House. In 1977, Carter invited Crosby, Stills & Nash to drop by. Or rather, Stephen Stills forced the issue.

"I loved Jimmy Carter," Stills said. "So I arranged [the meeting]. I'd paid my dues as a good party member. I knew who to call."

David Crosby claims they did more there than meet the president, however. "One of us, and I will not say who, lit a joint in the Oval Office, just to be able to say he'd done it, you know?" (Presumably, Carter was not there at the time.)

As for the actual meeting with the president, Graham Nash was moved by the moment, but more mundane concerns soon brought him back to Earth. "It was an interesting experience," he said. "I got a nice feeling from the man, but of course, very quickly, in true politician fashion, he tried to get us to commit to doing a concert for him."

Willie catches up with former President Carter in 1985. *Thomas S. England/ Time & Life Pictures/ Getty Images*

IT'S A
FAMILY
AFFAIR

WAS FRANK ZAPPA THE PROGENY OF CHILDREN'S TV?

LEAD "MOTHER" THE SON OF TV'S MR. GREEN JEANS? EVEN CAPTAIN KANGAROO WOULDN'T JUMP TO THAT CONCLUSION.

Never underestimate the credulity of rock fans, especially when confessions and/or clues about private details of performers' lives are placed *right there on the record*. (See the "Paul McCartney is dead" myth.)

One of the crazier stories to emerge from the singularly strange career of composer, bandleader, iconoclast, and rock guitar god Frank Zappa is that he was the son of Mr. Green Jeans, a character on the long-running kids' TV show *Captain Kangaroo*. The evidence? An instrumental track on Zappa's 1969 album *Hot Rats* called "Son of Mr. Green Genes" [*sic*]. That title just about sews it up, no?

No.

Zappa was, in fact, the son of Francis Vincent Zappa Sr., a Sicilian immigrant whose U.S. Defense Department jobs (along with Frank's poor health) took the family from Baltimore to Florida and later to various locations in California. The younger Zappa believed his real name to be Francis Vincent Zappa Jr., even going so far as to list it as such on some of his early albums. But when applying for a passport while in his mid-twenties, he had to submit his birth certificate, which, he was surprised to discover, listed his first name only as Frank.

Francis was "a name I always hated," Zappa wrote in his 1989 memoir, *The Real Frank Zappa Book*, adding that he was delighted to find a name other than that one on the document. Although, as he noted, "'Frank' isn't much of a bargain," either.

Zappa plays the Newport Jazz Festival, 1969. *David Redfern/Redferns/ Getty Images*

Mr. Green Jeans, meanwhile, was a character created by Hugh "Lumpy" Brannum. He played the genial handyman (as well as other characters) on *Captain Kangaroo* from 1955 to 1984.

Brannum was born in Sandwich, Illinois, and, after attending high school in suburban Chicago and college at the University of Redlands in California, played bass in various bands. He served in the Marines during World War II, and, following the war, joined Fred Waring and His Pennsylvanians. It was on Waring's radio show that Brannum met Bob Keeshan, who would later hire him for *Captain Kangaroo*. But before that, Brannum hosted a children's TV show in New York City called Uncle Lumpy's Cabin.

Mr. Green Jeans' name derived from his wardrobe, which was, as you might guess, green. Originally, he wore a pair of farmer's overalls, later moving to jeans and a denim jacket. The greenness of his clothes had to be taken as an article of faith by *Captain Kangaroo*'s audience, however, as the show wasn't broadcast in color until 1958.

Brannum's folksy, friendly character was "an extension of [his] real personality," Keeshan said in Brannum's *New York Times* obituary. (Brannum died in 1987.) But it was also drawn from stories about a farm boy named Little Orley that Brannum told on Waring's radio show and on a series of recordings made under the name Uncle Lumpy.

The myth connecting Zappa and Brannum took on enough of a life of its own that Zappa felt compelled to address it on the very first page of *The Real Frank Zappa Book*. "Because I recorded a song called 'Son of Mr. Green Genes' on the *Hot Rats* album in 1969," he wrote, "people have believed for years that the character with that name on the Captain Kangaroo TV show (played by *Lumpy Brannum*) was my 'real' Dad. No, he was not."

An earlier version of the track, titled "Mr. Green Genes," appeared on Zappa's previous album, *Uncle Meat*. It's a vocal number that begins with instructions to eat green vegetables, such as beans and celery, so as to stay, um, regular. Later the lyrics become more absurd, adding shoes, a garbage truck, and even the garbage truck's driver to the menu.

Zappa was a tireless recycler of concepts and musical themes, so it's not surprising that the music was modified and used again; nor was it unusual that the title of the successive tune, "Son of Mr. Green Genes," uses the parlance of monster movies (e.g., *Son of Frankenstein*, *Son of Dracula*, etc.), which Zappa loved.

Whoever started the myth seems to have missed that detail—to say nothing of the different spellings of the character's name and the name in the song title. But then, as Zappa once said, "Stupidity . . . is the basic building block of the universe." ✖

Driven by horns and a classic Frank Zappa guitar solo, "Son of Mr. Green Genes" is typical of the material on his mostly instrumental album, *Hot Rats*. The 1969 effort is Zappa's first release without the backing of the Mothers and is widely regarded as one of the first jazz-rock records.

MYTH TRACK

CHAPTER 35

WEIRD AL YANKOVIC—WHO'S HIS DADDY?

MASTER PARODIST THE SON OF POLKA KING FRANKIE YANKOVIC? THAT'S A BUNCH OF (MY) BOLOGNA.

Like father, like son? Not quite. Frankie Yankovic, circa 1960. GAB Archive/ Redferns/Getty Images

The late polka great Frankie Yankovic had three children from his two marriages. And none of them was named Weird Al.

Nevertheless, the world assumed that Weird Al Yankovic was indeed the progeny of Frankie, who won the first-ever Grammy Award for polka music and released more than two hundred recordings during his career, selling more than 30 million copies.

The mistake was understandable, of course. Both men played the accordion, and Weird Al has populated his parody music with plenty of polkas, including medleys of popular hits set to polka beats. And neither man particularly minded the association. "People always assumed I was his son, and he would never deny it," recalls Weird Al. "He would say, 'Oh yeah, that's my boy!'"

The mistake did not often work in the younger Yankovic's favor, however. The Lynwood, California, native started playing accordion the day before his sixth birthday, after a traveling salesman offered his parents a choice of accordion or guitar lessons for their son. He modeled himself after the senior Yankovic and Lawrence Welk's squeezebox specialist, Myron Floren. But after syndicated radio host Dr. Demento started playing his parodies of the Knack's "My Sharona" ("My Bologna") and Queen's "Another One Bites the Dust" ("Another One Rides the Bus") and Weird Al began playing shows, he noticed that some of Frankie's crowd began showing up—and were not happy with what they heard.

"On my first concert tour, I could always tell," Weird Al says. "After ten minutes there'd be the blue-haired women in the front row who'd be walking out because they obviously thought I was Frankie's kid and I was going to be playing polka music all night long. They'd hear the first rock 'n' roll power chord from the guitar and be like, 'Nope, this isn't Frankie's kid.' That followed me for a long time."

The two accordion men met in 1986, when CBS hired Weird Al to host a special segment for its pre–Grammy Awards telecast in anticipation of the first polka prize. "We did a whole segment called 'Frankie Goes to Hollywood,' and we gave him the whole kind of mock star on the Hollywood Walk of Fame, the whole poolside interview, and had a lot of fun," remembers Weird Al, who guested on "Who Stole the Kishka?" on Frankie's *Songs of the Polka King, Vol. 1* album in 1996. "It was a great way for us to finally meet each other."

What wasn't so fun, however, was when Frankie died of heart failure in Florida on October 14, 1998, at the age of eighty-three. "I got a call from someone who'd heard the news that Frankie had died," Yankovic says, "and this person said, 'I'm so sorry to hear that your father's dead.' And of course I was shocked and a bit freaked out and wasn't too happy this person hadn't fact checked before horrifying me with that statement. And NBC network news that night reported Frankie's death and said, 'He's gone, but his music lives on in his son, Weird Al Yankovic.' Nooooo! You're wrong! That was pretty horrible, you know?" ✖

"Nope, this isn't Frankie's kid." Weird Al in Las Vegas, 1999. *Jeff Kravitz/ FilmMagic, Inc./ Getty Images*

Weird Al may not be the biological son of Frankie Yankovic, but it's always fun when he claims his elder's polka-king mantle. Often, Al's versions of current rock and pop tunes done polka style have proven more durable than the original songs themselves. That's not necessarily the case with "Polkas on 45" from his second album, 1984's *Weird Al in 3-D*, on which he surveys Devo's "Jocko Homo," Deep Purple's "Smoke on the Water," the Beatles' "Hey Jude," and Iron Butterfly's "In-A-Gadda-Da-Vida," among other classics.

MYTH TRACK

WHAT'S THE STORY WITH THE WHITE STRIPES' "BROTHER-SISTER" ACT?

**JACK WHITE FELL IN LOVE WITH A GIRL—
EVEN THOUGH SHE WAS HIS "SISTER."**

When John "Jack" Gillis met Meg White, she was working at Memphis Smoke, a barbecue restaurant in the Detroit suburb of Royal Oak, Michigan, and he was playing guitar in the Detroit band Two-Star Tabernacle (after drumming in Goober & the Peas) and running his own Third Man Upholstery shop.

Within months they'd be husband and wife, although as far as the world was concerned once they started their own group, the White Stripes, they were brother and sister.

The sibling myth would be part of the White Stripes' lore throughout the group's nearly fourteen-year career. They'd refer to each other that way in interviews. Jack would introduce Meg as either his "sister" or "big sister" on stage, even as late as the duo's final tour, a 2007 swing through Canada documented in the 2010 film *Under Great White Northern Lights*. Jack explained to *Rolling Stone* in 2005, "If we had presented ourselves in another fashion . . . how would we have been perceived, right off the bat? When you see a band that is two pieces, husband and wife, boyfriend and girlfriend, you think, 'Oh, I see. . .' When they're brother and sister, you go, 'Oh, that's interesting.' You care more about the music, not the relationship."

The couple married on September 21, 1996, after a short courtship. The wedding was small and quickly planned. Meg wore white lace and daisies

Mated for life. Meg and Jack White, 2003.
Dimitri Hakke/Redferns/Getty Images

in her hair and went barefoot. Jack took her surname. They started playing music together immediately—"Meg had never played drums before, so it was really fresh and unusual," Jack said—and on July 14, 1997, they performed their first public gig as the White Stripes (while Jack was still logging time in Two-Star Tabernacle and another band, the Go). The Stripes' stripped-down, rootsy cacophony caught the imaginations of hipsters at home and

The White Stripes play the Reading Festival, 2002. *Nicky J. Sims/Redferns/ Getty Images*

abroad, and by the time of their third album, 2001's *White Blood Cells*, they were on the charts and had gold and platinum records to hang on their walls.

By then the world started to catch on that the sibling association was an act. They had, in fact, divorced in March 2000, though Jack considered Meg and himself "mated for life." Even after enterprising reporters back in Detroit, who knew the real story all along, produced copies of the marriage license and divorce certificate, the duo continued the façade, and some still bought it. *The New Yorker* famously referred to the duo as "two siblings from Detroit" even as other publications were, at the very least, qualifying their claimed relationship. And the Flaming Lips slyly referenced them as brother and sister in the 2003 song "Thank You Jack White (For the Fiber-Optic Jesus That You Gave Me)."

In 2002, Jack told *Spin* magazine that he and Meg had "given up" any pretense of . . . well, anything. "People can say whatever they want at this point," he said. "It never mattered to us. We were never trying to create this. We were never trying to be icons or hoping to get attention. We never purposefully sat down and said, 'If we say these things, people will talk about us.'" He also emphasized that "in the end, twenty years from now, the only thing that matters about any band is if the music was good."

The music was good, and the Stripes only got bigger after 2003's *Elephant* album went double platinum and became the first of three consecutive

Top 10 albums on the Billboard 200 chart, thanks in part to the chart-topping hit "Seven Nation Army." The group also won four Grammy Awards before calling it quits on February 2, 2011, with a note on their website telling fans the split was "for a myriad of reasons, but mostly to preserve what is beautiful and special about the band and have it stay that way. . . . The White Stripes do not belong to Meg and Jack anymore. The White Stripes belong to you now and you can do with it whatever you want. The beauty of art and music is that it can last forever if people want it to."

Jack and Meg both remarried. Jack wed British model Karen Elson, who appeared in the Stripes' "Blue Orchid" video, on June 1, 2005, in Manaus, Brazil, with Meg as maid of honor. In June 2011 the couple announced their divorce, throwing a party to celebrate "the making and breaking of the sacred union of marriage" and pledging to remain "dear and trusted friends and co-parents" to their two children. Jack, who now makes his home in Nashville, continues to play in the bands the Raconteurs and the Dead Weather and runs the Third Man record label (which released an album by Elson), retail store, and recording studio.

Meg, meanwhile, married Jackson Smith, son of Patti Smith and the late MC5 guitarist Fred "Sonic" Smith, in May 2009 in Jack's backyard in Nashville. She has laid low in recent years—her bout of acute anxiety forced the Stripes to cancel a bunch of concerts in 2007—doing a bit of modeling and photography. She was also the inspiration for Ray LaMontagne's song "Meg White" from his 2008 album, *Gossip in the Grain*. ✘

Few had heard of the White Stripes or cared if Jack and Meg were siblings, dating, or divorced in the spring of 1998 when the duo released their first single, "Let's Shake Hands"—although by that time they'd certainly done a little more than what the title implies. The original seven-inch single, whose first 500 copies were printed on red vinyl, has the raw energy of the Stripes getting their heads around a concept that would blossom into one of the most original and provocative rock sounds of the '90s and early 2000s.

MYTH TRACK

37

REALLY? KEITH RICHARDS HAD A SNORT OF HIS DAD'S EARTHLY REMAINS?

"ASHES TO ASHES . . . [SNOOOOOOOOOORK]."
THE HUMAN RIFF EXHIBITS A RARE FORM OF FILIAL PIETY.

There isn't much in the way of drugs that Keith Richards hasn't smoked, shot, or snorted. As much as he may look like a casualty of his intemperance—indeed, his deeply creased visage may be the *Picture of Dorian Gray* for the entire baby boom generation—he's somehow lived to tell the tale.

But there's one thing the gnarled guitar hero has put up his nose that may not have occurred to . . . well, anyone in history, really. Originally, Richards told the story on himself, but when the outcry over the alleged incident reached a fever pitch, he withdrew it, after which it became just another chapter in his long legacy as the embodiment of rock's insatiable, indestructible spirit.

Perhaps there's a statute of limitations on outrage, however, because when it came time to write his autobiography—which he called, simply, *Life*—Richards set the record straight, admitting that yes, he'd actually lined up a rail of his late father's ashes and snorted them.

The episode began innocently enough (relatively speaking—this *is* Keith Richards we're talking about), when *New Musical Express* scribe Mark Beaumont asked him to expound on his worst drug experience. The answer was that he once took some drugs that were laced with strychnine, leaving him semicomatose, aware of his surroundings, but unable to speak or move.

But then the Rolling Stones guitarist volunteered this: "The strangest thing I've tried to snort? My father. I snorted my father. He was cremated, and I couldn't resist grinding him up with a little bit of blow. My dad wouldn't have cared, he didn't give a shit. It went down pretty well, and I'm still alive."

Keef, always at home in the tabloids. *New York Daily News Archive via Getty Images*

DAILY ◉ NEWS

NEW YORK'S HOMETOWN NEWSPAPER   NYDailyNews.com

50¢

LUPICA:
Rudy's wives tales
SEE PAGE 4

I SNORTED MY DAD

SEE PAGE 3

Keith Richards

GETTY IMAGES

Stones' Richards says he mixed father's ashes with cocaine, but Keith's manager claims it was all 'in jest'

The response to Richards' claim was instantaneous and unfavorable. "There were headlines, editorials, there were op-eds on cannibalism, there was some of the old flavor of Street of Shame indignation at the Stones," Richards wrote in *Life*. "[The BBC's] John Humphreys on prime-time radio was heard to ask, 'Do you think Keith Richards has gone too far *this* time?'"

The controversy even caused ripples of discomfort at Disney, the company behind the film *Pirates of the Carribbean* franchise, in which Richards played the father of Johnny Depp's character, Captain Jack Sparrow. A company vice president commented that when he heard the story, he wondered, "How are we going to spin this?" adding, "Keith won't be doing a lot of publicity for this movie."

It's not like Richards to pull back from his actions, however controversial. After all, this is the guy who, during the trial for the infamous 1967 bust at his Redlands estate, told the court, "We are not old men. We are not worried about petty morals."

But pull back he did, in a posting on the Rolling Stones' website the day after the ash-snorting story broke. Stones spokesman Bernard Doherty, meanwhile, claimed, "It was an off-the-cuff remark, a joke, and it's not true. File under April Fool's joke."

But once told, as we've seen, certain stories can't really be taken back—and this is one of them. And whether it was true or not, the snort heard 'round the world became inseparable from Richards' life of legendary excess, so much so that the truth was bound to come out sooner or later.

In *Life*, Richards recalled a note he had drafted and sent to his manager, Jane Rose: "The truth of the matter is that after having Dad's ashes in a black box for six years, because I really couldn't bring myself to scatter him to the winds, I finally planted a sturdy English oak to spread him around. And as I took the lid off of the box, a fine spray of his ashes blew out onto the table. I couldn't just brush him off, so I wiped my finger over it and snorted the residue. Ashes to ashes, father to son. He is now growing oak trees and would love me for it."

Richards told the tale again to *CBS Sunday Morning* reporter Anthony Mason, adding a bit of anthropological justification for his actions. "Ingesting your ancestors has been a very, very important thing throughout history," he said. "Many ancient cultures do that. I mean—'Hey, Dad!'—I wouldn't eat him, but I snorted him. Just a little bit. He's on the table, what am I gonna do, brush him off?"

Mason asked him how it made him feel. "It got me off," Richards said with a laugh. "It was a bit gritty, actually. But it was done and it was done. I couldn't let the man go to waste." ✖

Richards, not worried about "petty morals" in June 1967, around the time of his first drug trial. *Sherman/Getty Images*

Booze and pills and powders, you can choose your medicine/Well here's another goodbye to another good friend," Keith Richards sings on "Before They Make Me Run." The song seems tailor-made for his unique send-off of his father's ashes, but in fact it appeared decades before, on the Rolling Stones' 1978 album, *Some Girls*. Still, it's one of the definitive anthems of surviving the rock 'n' roll lifestyle and staying one step ahead of the forces that oppose it.

EAT TO THE BEAT

38

DID MICK JAGGER EAT A MARS BAR LODGED YOU KNOW WHERE?

A SWEET PREMISE, BUT CALORICALLY (AND FACTUALLY) EMPTY.

Mick Jagger once proclaimed himself, in song, as "a man of wealth and taste." And that taste, according to one popular story, included an interesting manner of consuming a candy bar.

The chocolate-covered myth stems from an equally infamous incident in the Rolling Stones' history. On February 12, 1967, guitarist Keith Richards' moated, fifteenth-century home, Redlands, in West Wittering, England, was raided by British police, who had been tipped off by editors at the *News of the World*—as retribution for Jagger threatening to sue the tabloid over another story—about a weekend party that would include a substantial quantity of drugs, primarily LSD. Word spread that when police entered the premises, they found a relatively sedate scene—save for Jagger reportedly eating a Mars bar that had been lodged in the vagina of then-girlfriend Marianne Faithfull—who, by the way, was wearing only a fur rug and subsequently bared all for the *gendarme*.

A number of elements of the tale were, in fact, true. The fur rug. The flashing. Jagger and Faithfull together. And there was even a Mars bar present. It was not, however, being eaten anywhere, much less from Faithfull's nether regions.

Faithfull wrote in her 1994 memoir, *Faithfull: An Autobiography*, "The story went like this: a group of dissolute rock stars lured an innocent girl to a remote cottage where, having plied her with drugs, they had their way with her, including various sex acts involving a Mars bar. . . . The Mars bar was a very effective piece of demonizing. *Way* out there. It was so overdone, with such malicious twisting of the facts. Mick retrieving a Mars bar from my vagina, indeed! It was far too jaded for us even to have conceived of. It was a dirty old man's fantasy. . . . A cop's idea of what people do on acid!"

Isn't it romantic? Mick and Marianne in the gardens at Sydney's Mount St. Margaret Hospital after her 1969 overdose. *Lipman/The Sydney Morning Herald/ Fairfax Media via Getty Images*

Mick and Marianne share a moment—but not a candy bar—in 1967. *Hulton Archive/Getty Images*

Rest assured, however, that Faithfull was by no means an "innocent girl" at the time of the bust. She was seventeen years old and attending convent school when Stones manager/producer Andrew Loog Oldham met her at a party in 1964. Her father was a philology professor, while her mother was a ballet dancer and Austrian baroness. Jagger did not make a good first impression. At the aforementioned party, he spilled a glass of champagne (allegedly on purpose) on Faithfull and then wiped her breasts with his hand. Faithfull was, according to friend Barry Miles, "really disgusted" by the whole Stones camp at first. "She thought they looked greasy and sort of disgusting," Miles said.

She was, however, open to Oldham's suggestion that she become a singer. The manager got Jagger and Richards to write her a song, and the result, melodic and purposefully chaste, "As Tears Go By" became a Top 10 hit in the United Kindgom. Faithfull went on to dally with Richards and the Stones' other guitarist, Brian Jones, but Jagger was smitten with her, wooing Faithfull—who at the time was married to art gallery owner John Dunbar—and ultimately dumping his own fiancée, Chrissie Shrimpton.

Jagger and Faithfull were in the early stages of their relationship at the time of the Redlands bust. Identified as "Miss X" in the police report, Faithfull was wearing the rug—which Richards described in his autobiography, *Life*, as "made of pelts of some kind, rabbit"—after taking a bath, though, Richards joked that the amount of her body covered made her "quite chastely attired for once."

The Mars bar? "There was one on the table," Richards confirmed, "because on acid suddenly you get sugar lack, and you're munching away." Richards contends, however, that Jagger was not doing so when the police entered the house—with Faithfull or otherwise.

"How that connotation came about and how the press managed to make a Mars bar on a table and Marianne wrapped in a fur rug into a myth is kind of classic," Richards wrote. "The evening paper headlines are 'Naked Girl at Stones Party.' Info directly from the police. But the Mars bar as a dildo? That's a rather large leap." As Stones biographer Philip Norman pointed out in 1984's *Symphony for the Devil: The Rolling Stones Story* that "the Mars bar was a detail of such sheer madness as to make the story believed, then and forever after."

Jagger and Richards were charged with possession of drugs among other things in the Redlands incident and spent one night in jail; Jagger claimed to have heard about the Mars bar rumor from another inmate, and then passed the story along to Faithfull. Both Stones were found guilty, and Judge Leslie Block, who pronounced the two rock stars as "scum and filth," sentenced Jagger to a fine and three months in jail, while Richards was fined and sentenced to a year behind bars. After public outcry, including an editorial in the *London Times* asking "Who Breaks a Butterfly on a Wheel?," the Lord Chief Justice of the London Appeal Court dismissed Richards' charges and gave Jagger a conditional discharge. The Glimmer Twins wrote "We Love You" for the Stones as an expression of thanks for the public support.

Jagger and Faithfull remained a couple into 1970; she miscarried in November 1968 and then attempted suicide after Brian Jones' death on July 3, 1969. They split up during the spring of 1970, when Jagger decided to move to France for tax purposes, and on the day he married Bianca Perez Moreno de Macias (May 12, 1971), Faithfull was arrested for drunk and disorderly conduct. She's continued her recording career as well, including the 2011 release *Horses and High Heels*. She also penned a second book, *Memories, Dreams and Reflections*, in 2007. ✖

Either of the two versions of "As Tears Go By"—Marianne Faithfull's 1964 original, which Mick Jagger and Keith Richards wrote expressly for her, or the Rolling Stones' 1965 treatment, which was a Top 10 hit in the United States the following year.

MYTH TRACK

CHAPTER 39

DID MAMA CASS ELLIOT CHOKE TO DEATH ON A HAM SANDWICH?

THE TRUTH BEHIND THE COLDEST CUT OF ALL.

In some ways, the story seems too plausible not to believe: Mama Cass Elliot, who at the time of her death at age thirty-two stood five-foot-five and weighed 225 pounds (but may have once weighed as much as 300), succumbed not to the stereotypical rock star death by drug overdose but, according to legend, by choking on a ham sandwich. It's a fate that seems part and parcel of her being a person of size who indulged her outsize appetites.

But the truth is more complicated, and considerably murkier, for the Mamas & the Papas' most recognizable member.

Born Ellen Naomi Cohen, Elliot was already heavyset in her youth. Precocious and gifted with a high IQ, she once vowed, "I'm gonna be the most famous fat girl who ever lived." She adopted her stage name—stories abound as to how she chose it—when she made the leap from her hometown of Baltimore to New York.

She was already known as Mama Cass by the time she recorded with Tim Rose and James Hendricks in the folk group the Big Three. Later she joined the Mugwumps, which included Hendricks, Zal Yanovsky (later of the Lovin' Spoonful), and Denny Doherty, who would play a role in her next group. When the Mugwumps broke up, Doherty signed on with John Phillips and his wife, Michelle, in the New Journeymen. At Doherty's insistence, Elliot was included, too, and they became the Mamas & the Papas.

The group was a sensation thanks to the epochal folk-pop hits "California Dreamin'" and "Monday, Monday." But their union was relatively short-lived, thanks in part to personal issues between band members. Doherty was carrying on an affair with Michelle Phillips, while Elliot's love for Doherty went unrequited. Tensions were already running high in the group, and when Phillips outraged Elliot by insulting her in front of Mick Jagger at a party, she quit.

The Mamas and the Papas, circa 1968. *Michael Ochs Archives/Getty Images*

As a solo artist, Elliot hit with "Dream a Little Dream of Me" (originally a Mamas & Papas track), as well as "California Earthquake" and "Make Your Own Kind of Music." She bombed as a mainroom attraction in Las Vegas, however, and stayed in the spotlight by appearing on TV game shows and variety shows, even sitting in for Johnny Carson occasionally on *The Tonight Show*.

In the meantime, she established herself as the "queen of the L.A. pop scene." Her Laurel Canyon home became the center of the musical universe where numerous artists wrote songs, sang together, or just hung out. Famously, it was there that David Crosby, Graham Nash, and Stephen Stills first harmonized, forming the basis for a musical partnership that still lives on today.

Though beloved by everyone, Elliot was perennially unlucky in her relationships, marrying twice and giving birth to a daughter, Owen. Her use of drugs, including heroin, debilitated her health and did her career no favors. But she achieved a personal milestone when she played a sold-out two-week engagement at the London Palladium in 1974.

At the end of the Palladium run, Elliot stayed out all night partying, including a stop at Jagger's thirty-second birthday bash. She returned to her apartment, a flat on loan from singer Harry Nilsson, and slept away most of the next day. Around noon, an assistant to Keith Moon (the Who drummer also used the place) entered the bedroom to collect some of Moon's clothes, but did not disturb Elliot. When Elliot still hadn't awakened by midafternoon, her personal assistant, Dot McLeod, and tour manager and quasi-boyfriend George Caldwell found her dead.

(In a macabre twist, Moon himself would die of a drug overdose in the same flat, four years later.)

MYTH TRACK

Named for a club in the Virgin Islands where the Mamas and the Papas came together as a quartet, "Creeque Alley" is the group's story of its own formation. The song appeared on the 1967 album *The Mamas and the Papas Deliver* and became a No. 5 single on the Billboard pop chart. Its pertinence to the death of Elliot has to do with the rather tacky last line of the song's chorus, a statement of fact that would later prove fatal: "And no one's getting fat except Mama Cass." She was comfortable with her size, though, and she belted out the lyric with gusto. But still . . . ouch.

The story that emerged from the scene was that Elliot had choked on a ham sandwich she was eating while lying in bed and aspirated her own vomit.' It was planted in the public consciousness first by Dr. Anthony Greenburgh, Elliot's private physician and a "doctor to the stars" on the London circuit, who was called in by Caldwell.

Not only did Greenburgh theorize about the sandwich, but he took pains to deny that drink or drugs were part of Elliot's life—never mind that he'd prescribed tranquilizers for her nerves only a few weeks prior and that she was probably drinking at the parties she attended in the hours before her death.

Elliot's biographer, Eddi Fiegel, writes that the room had been swept of drugs, including the tranquilizers and liquid cocaine, by Caldwell before Greenburgh arrived, essentially charging that the doctor was called in to offer a cover story.

Some see the fact that there *was* a ham sandwich in the room as a smoking gun, but it was only smoked pork. The police report, according to Fiegel, says that it was untouched.

And yet the confusion didn't even end there.

When an official autopsy was conducted, pathologist Professor Keith Simpson claimed that Elliot's death was not of natural causes but that further tests were needed. Coroner Gavin Thurston had the last word, however, asserting that she *did* die of natural causes—the result of "fatty myocardial degeneration due to obesity."

He went on to say there was nothing blocking her mouth or throat (thus busting the ham sandwich myth) and that there was no alcohol or drugs in her system (also cashiering the overdose theory).

"Her heart had just given out," her former musical compatriot John Phillips wrote in his own memoir, *Papa John*. "And that was some big heart." ✘

THE PIPE THAT HELPED MAMA CASS' PIPES

ACCORDING TO A POPULAR STORY, Elliot's vocal range increased by three notes after she was hit on the head with a metal pipe. The incident happened in the Virgin Islands, where the Mamas & the Papas were vacationing and coming together as a group. "It's true," she told *Rolling Stone* in 1968. "They were tearing this club apart . . . revamping it, putting in a dance floor. Workmen dropped a thin metal plumbing pipe and knocked me to the ground. I had a concussion and went to the hospital. I had a bad headache for about two weeks and all of a sudden I was singing higher. It's true. Honest to God."

40

DID FRANK ZAPPA DROP A LOAD ON STAGE . . . AND THEN EAT IT?

Musical genius and provocateur, yes. But public defecator? Frank Zappa, circa 1968. *Charlie Gillett/ Redferns/Getty Images*

SOMETHING SMELLS FUNNY ABOUT THIS ONE.

Frank Zappa was one of the more outrageous artists in rock history, and one who was never afraid to challenge society's accepted manners and morés. But even he had his limits.

One of the prevailing myths about the iconoclastic composer, bandleader, and guitarist is that he . . . well, let's let *him* tell it, as he did on the second page of his memoir, *The Real Frank Zappa Book*:

The . . . fantasy is that I once "took a shit on stage." This has been propounded with many variations, including (but not limited to):

[1] I ate shit on stage.
[2] I had a "gross-out contest" (what the fuck is a "gross-out contest"?) with Captain Beefheart and we both ate shit on stage.
[3] I had a "gross-out contest" with Alice Cooper and he stepped on baby chickens and then I ate shit on stage, etc.

That doesn't mean that Zappa didn't do things that were exceedingly outré onstage, especially in the early days of his band, Mothers of Invention.

"We did everything," Zappa told *Rolling Stone* in 1968. "We performed a couple of marriages on stage. We pulled people out of the audience and made them make speeches. One time we brought 30 people up on stage and some of them took our instruments and the rest of them sang 'Louie, Louie,' as we left.

Another popular feature of the show involved a stuffed giraffe equipped with a whipped cream–loaded hose running out its nether regions. "Ray Collins would go up to the giraffe and massage it with a frog hand puppet," Zappa said, "and then the giraffe's tail would stiffen and the first three rows of the audience would get sprayed with whipped cream shooting out of the hose. All with musical accompaniment, of course."

Zappa explained, "Music is always a commentary on society, and certainly the atrocities on stage are quite mild compared to those conducted in our behalf by our government. You can't write a chord ugly enough to say what you want to say sometimes, so you have to rely on a giraffe filled with whipped cream."

The first "atrocities" happened by chance, he said, when a group of Marines came to a show at the height of the Vietnam War and Zappa invited them onstage. Zappa said he threw the Marines a baby doll and told them to "pretend that this is a 'gook baby'" and "show the folks in the audience what you guys do for a living." The Marines tore the doll apart while the band played. After that, Zappa noted, "Nobody was laughing."

But, back to the defecation myth: Zappa may have helped instigate it by doing a photo shoot for an English magazine, the *International Times*, in which he's seated on a toilet, naked except for the pants around his ankles. The infamous shot later appeared as a popular poster, with Zappa even authorizing one version that contained the legend "Phi Zappa Krappa."

As for delivering dada in the form of dookie, however, it didn't happen, a fact that actually seems to disappoint some of his fans. As Zappa wrote in his book:

> *I was in a London club called the Speak Easy in 1967 or '68. A member of a group called the Flock . . . came over to me and said:* "You're fantastic. When I heard about you eating that shit on stage, I thought, 'That guy is **way, way out there.**'"
>
> *I said,* "I never ate shit on stage." *He looked really depressed—like I had just broken his heart.*
>
> *For the records, folks,* **I never took a shit on stage, and the closest I ever came to eating shit anywhere was at a Holiday Inn buffet in Fayetteville, North Carolina, in 1973.** ✖

41

DOES OZZY HAVE A TASTE FOR THINGS WITH WINGS?

DID THE PUTATIVE PRINCE OF DARKNESS REALLY BITE THE HEAD OFF A LIVE BAT?

The putative Prince of Darkness has often been accused—by critics, religious groups, and nervous parents everywhere—of being a rabid beast.

Not to worry, though—he's had his shots. Doctors orders, after Ozzy Osbourne perpetrated one of the most notorious, if unintentional, stunts in rock history.

On January 20, 1982, Osbourne performed at Veterans Memorial Auditorium in Des Moines, Iowa. The show, part of his *Diary of a Madman* tour, was filled with calculated outrage. Onstage antics included the (faux) hanging of a midget and the flinging of raw meat into the crowd.

Osbourne's fans—impressionable lot that they were—responded in kind, bringing various animal parts to concerts to fling back. In one case, at least, they brought a whole animal, albeit a tiny one.

Mark Neal, who was seventeen at the time, told the *Des Moines Register* that his brother had brought a live bat home from school one day and intended to keep it as a pet. Not surprisingly, the bat expired, and rather than dispose of it, Neal put the carcass in a baggie and snuck it into the show.

Ozzy, who was giving his usual maniacal performance and was no doubt fueled by his Herculean regimen of drink and drugs, saw the bat land on the stage. Assuming it was rubber (he says), he grabbed it and bit the head off.

Instantly he recognized his mistake.

As blood and rancid bat guts ran down his chin, Osbourne thought, "Oh, *fuck me*, I didn't just go and eat a fucking bat, did I?"

He did.

After the show, Osbourne was rushed to Broadlawns Medical Center for rabies shots, a regimen he had to continue for the rest of the tour.

News of the incident spread like wildfire, and fear and loathing followed Osbourne wherever he went. He was met with protests and pickets,

Ozzy offers up a cogent explanation of the bat incident, 1982. *Time & Life Pictures/Getty Images* was banned from certain venues, and ASPCA began monitoring his shows.

Fans, meanwhile, ate it up.

Perhaps not surprisingly, this was not Osbourne's only head-biting incident from that era. Some months before, Osbourne and his manager (and later, wife) Sharon Arden, met with Columbia Records executives in Los Angeles to get the label's support for his latest album. A pair of doves were procured with the intention that Ozzy would release them in the conference room and shout "rock 'n' roll!" so as to make an impression on the execs. Instead—and much to the horror of everyone in the room—he bit the head off of one of them, spewing blood and feathers around the room.

Osbourne was thrown out of the building.

Though clearly more outrageous, the dove incident hasn't stained the singer's reputation to quite the same degree as the bat biting. At the conclusion of his autobiography, *I Am Ozzy*, Osbourne writes that he has no illusions about what will be put on his headstone.

Ozzy Osbourne, born 1948.
Died, whenever.
He bit the head off a bat. ✘

One of Ozzy's lesser-known numbers, "Party with the Animals," appeared on the 1992 soundtrack for *Buffy the Vampire Slayer* and was also tacked onto the 2002 reissue of *No More Tears*. It's probably really about partying with groupies— "no dogs allowed," Ozzy sings at one point, though he notes in his autobiography that that was never really a sticking point for him. But we're trying to imagine a real party, thrown by Ozzy, with real animals. And we're imagining that any animals in attendance would be very nervous.

MYTH TRACK

CHAPTER 42

WHAT'S UP WITH VAN HALEN AND M&Ms?

GIVE THEM ANYTHING YOU WANT BACKSTAGE, BUT SERVE THE BROWN ONES AT YOUR OWN PERIL.

Unusual and outrageous contract demands are an integral part of rock 'n' roll lore. The bigger they come, the odder they are, it seems.

But the one that takes the cake—or at least the candy—is Van Halen and its curious aversion to brown M&Ms.

During the late '70s and early '80s, the hard rock group's original lineup—with frontman David Lee Roth playing a flamboyant foil to guitar hero Eddie Van Halen—rode a wave of multiplatinum smashes such as *Van Halen*, *Van Halen II*, *Women and Children First*, *Fair Warning*, *Diver Down*, and *1984*. Radio was pumping anthems like "Runnin' with the Devil," "Ain't Talkin' 'Bout Love," "Dance the Night Away," and "And the Cradle Will Rock," and covers of the Kinks' "You Really Got Me," Roy Orbison's "(Oh) Pretty Woman," and Martha & the Vandellas' "Dancing in the Street."

All of that made Van Halen a certified concert attraction, jumping off an opening spot for Black Sabbath after its first album was released and attaining arena headline status on its own. The band also put in an appearance at the 1983 US Festival near San Bernardino, California, netting the group $1.5 million, certified by the *Guinness Book of World Records* as the highest single appearance fee ever paid.

Van Halen was money in the bank for promoters, meaning the group was in high demand and could ask for most anything it wanted. And turning the pages of its contract rider, many show producers found that one thing the group wanted in its dressing room was M&Ms.

But not the brown ones.

David Lee Roth backstage in the early '80s—presumably ranting about something other than M&Ms. *Chris Walter/ WireImage/Getty Images*

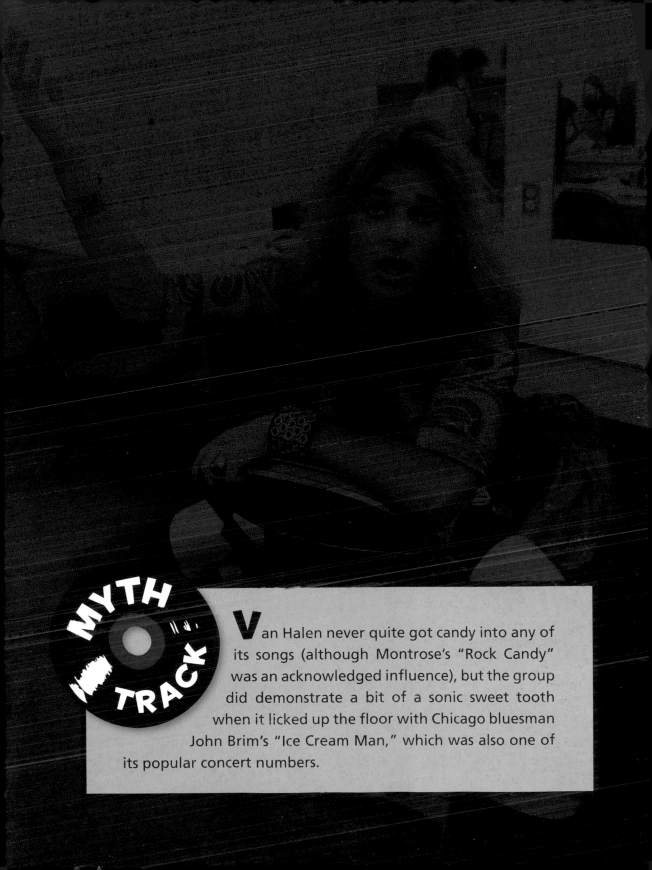

Van Halen never quite got candy into any of its songs (although Montrose's "Rock Candy" was an acknowledged influence), but the group did demonstrate a bit of a sonic sweet tooth when it licked up the floor with Chicago bluesman John Brim's "Ice Cream Man," which was also one of its popular concert numbers.

ARMADILLO PRESENTS

VAN HALEN

PLUS

THE BUGS HENDERSON GROUP

featuring LYNN GROOM

MON. JULY 3

THOUGH VAN HALEN'S FAMOUS M&M RIDER REQUIREMENT has risen to the top of the heap, the rock annals are filled with rider demands that range from sensible, to curious, to hilarious. Aerosmith, for example, has banned Wonder Bread and Pakistani pressed towels (whatever those are) from their backstage area. Axl Rose, on the other hand, has specifically demanded Wonder Bread and insisted on Solo brand paper cups only. (His Guns N' Roses bandmates were less complex, basically asking for the four rock 'n' roll food groups: salty snacks, booze, smokes, and an "assortment of adult magazines.") In 2002, Sheryl Crow's people outlined the tour's specific alcoholic needs for each day of the week (Wednesday was Courvosier day).

For sheer reading enjoyment, however, it's hard to imagine any rider surpassing that crafted by Iggy and the Stooges crew chief Jos Grain for one of the band's European tours. First revealed to the public on The Smoking Gun website, the document is filled with hilarious asides, one-liners, and witticisms, including Grain's idea for a reality TV show (which was attached to the rider as an addendum). Describing the band's very rigorous and lengthy onstage requirements, for example, Grain asks promoters, "For the sidefills [monitor speakers at the side of the stage], can we have two great big enormous things, please, of a type that might be venerated as gods by the inhabitants of the Easter Islands, reaching volumes that would make Beelzebub soil his underpants?"

For the record, some other unusual backstage rider requests:

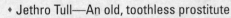

- Jethro Tull—An old, toothless prostitute
- Mariah Carey, Sting, and Mary J. Blige—expensive designer candles
- The Black Crowes—A bag of marijuana
- Paul McCartney—No meat
- Janet Jackson—A brand-new toilet seat
- Jefferson Starship—Nuclear warheads

It's been portrayed, of course, as an epic exercise in ego and power, evidence of a group whose self-importance had grown out of control. Plain or peanut is one thing, but banning a particular color? It seemed . . . unnecessary, especially since Van Halen promised that the presence of any of the offending candies "anywhere in the backstage area or immediate vicinity" could result in "pain of forfeiture of the show with full compensation." Meaning someone would have more than chocolate on their hands if it went down that way.

The group, however, claims that there was a purpose behind this particular madness—or, as Roth explained in his 1997 autobiography, *Crazy from the Heat*, "things are not what they seem." According to Roth, the demand stemmed from experience in primarily smaller markets where less-experienced promoters would not read the group's contract carefully enough, missing key safety and technical guidelines more than backstage niceties. "The contract rider read like a version of the Chinese Yellow Pages because there was so much equipment, and so many human beings to make it function," Roth wrote. So the brown M&Ms clause became "a little test" to make sure the promoters were paying proper attention.

"When I would walk backstage, if I saw a brown M&M in that bowl . . . well, line-check the entire production. Guaranteed you're going to arrive at a technical error. They didn't read the contract. Guaranteed you'd run into a problem. Sometimes it would threaten to just destroy the whole show. Something like, literally, life-threatening." By way of example he wrote about a college concert in Pueblo, Colorado, where, he (a) found a brown M&M and (b) the stage literally sank through the flooring of the arena because the organizers had not heeded the contract's weight requirements.

Of course, Roth added to the M&M mystique by going "into full Shakespearan 'What is *this* before me?' . . . and promptly trashed the dressing room. Dumped the buffet, kicked a hole in the door, twelve hundred dollars' worth of fun." In the press, however, the figure grew to $85,000 in backstage damages. But, as Roth wrote, "Who am I to get in the way of a good rumor?"

Van Halen bassist Michael Anthony later noted, "The brown M&Ms thing served a purpose, but it kind of bit us in the ass. People thought it was just us making some big, superstar demands and didn't know about the technical stuff. So we were assholes with big egos."

Some promoters who did pay close attention to the contract chose to have a little fun with Van Halen's request. More than a few have claimed that they removed all of the other colors *except* brown, leaving bowls of them conspicuously around the backstage area. And during one of his tours, Billy Squier included a rider clause requesting the brown M&Ms that promoters had removed for Van Halen's shows. ✖

DOCTOR, DOCTOR,

GIMME

THE NEWS

CHAPTER 43

DID KEITH RICHARDS REALLY GET THE FLUSH 'N' FILL?

DID KEEF LET IT BLEED FOR A SECRET MEDICAL PROCEDURE IN SWITZERLAND?

It's one of rock's most infamous and tantalizing myths: Keith Richards traveled to Switzerland in the early '70s to kick heroin by having his blood completely drained and replenished. Keith says he didn't; others say he did. Trouble is, everyone's stories seem to be as full of holes as a piece of, well, Swiss cheese.

"The lifeblood of good conspiracies is that you'll never find out," Richards wrote in his 2010 autobiography, *Life*; "the lack of evidence keeps them fresh. No one's ever going to find out if I had my blood changed or not. The story is well beyond the reach of evidence or, if it never happened, my denials."

While he was making the rounds promoting *Life*, Richards appeared on TV's *CBS Sunday Morning*, where he was asked about the story by interviewer Anthony Mason. "I created the myth," Richards said. "It's all my own work." He claimed he was on the way to Switzerland to kick his debilitating heroin habit (presumably in another fashion) and, pursued at the airport by paparazzi who wanted to know what he was up to, made up a story.

"I said 'I'm gonna get my blood changed,'" Richards said he told them. "I just wanted 'em off my back. So I just spun a yarn. I'm still living with it."

Besides, he concluded with bravado, "I wouldn't swap this blood for nobody."

So that's it, then. The "vampire myth," bloody good tale though it is, is untrue.

Well, not so fast.

This much is certain: At the time the blood transfusion allegedly took place, the Rolling Stones were about to go on their 1973 tour of Europe. For Richards to survive the rigors of performing—never mind the

Rock's indefatigable, indestructible man, circa 1974. *Keystone France/ Gamma Keystone via Getty Images*

"Connection," a Rolling Stones song featured on their 1967 album *Between the Buttons*, is ostensibly about a romantic relationship and the rigors of rock 'n' roll travel. But it could just as well be about drugs, their lack of availability on the road, and the difficulties of smuggling them from country to country.

The Human Riff in Honolulu, 1973. *Robert Knight Archive/ Redferns/Getty Images*

complications of crossing borders, smuggling drugs, making new connections in foreign lands, etc.—he knew he had to get off of heroin, and in very short order.

The story of how he did it may have initially sprung from the line he tossed off in that Swiss airport, but it got legs in 1979 when Tony Sanchez (a.k.a. Spanish Tony), Richards' former aid and drug supplier, published a notorious tell-all memoir titled *Up and Down with the Rolling Stones.*

Sanchez claims Richards heard of the controversial cure from Marshall Chess, the son of Chess Records cofounder Leonard Chess and the man tapped to run Rolling Stones Records, who was himself a junkie.

Sanchez wrote that Chess told Richards, "There's a doctor in Florida who can get you off dope in a few days by changing your blood. He did it for me in Mexico a while back, and it worked perfectly."

Arrangements were made for the doctor—identified as Dr. Denber by Sanchez—to perform the blood change in Villars-sur-Ollon, Switzerland, after the Stones tour left England and hit the continent. Chess, Sanchez claims, would take the cure at the same time.

Sanchez's tale is incredibly detailed. He has actual figures for the doctor's fee ($5,000, plus expenses) and how much Richards' rented villa cost. He claims Richards offered to pay for him to go through the procedure as well, but, frightened by the radical procedure, he declined.

Significantly, though, he left Switzerland, returned to England, and was not present when the alleged cure took place. But Richards described it to him, he says, when Sanchez rejoined the tour in Munich.

"It's quite simple, really," Sanchez wrote, quoting Richards. "He just changed our blood little by little so that there was no heroin in our bodies after forty-eight hours. There was no pain at all, and we spent the rest of the week just resting and building our strength up."

Sanchez claimed that Richards was back on drugs immediately after the procedure, regarding its success as something of a safety net. "It doesn't matter if I get hooked again now," Richards told him. "I can give it up any time I like without any bother."

Sanchez claimed, earnestly or not, that struck a bad chord with him. He may have been Richards' drug supplier and the facilitator of all manner of mischief in the guitarist's life, but he still knew when a line was being crossed. Sanchez wrote, "I couldn't help wondering where all this blood was coming from or resenting the decadence of debauched millionaires regaining the health, vampirelike, from the fresh, clean blood of innocents."

In his 1992 biography of Richards, Victor Bockris describes the "blood clean[ing]" procedure in greater detail: "The treatment involved a hemodialysis process in which the patient's blood was passed through a pump, where it was separated from sterile dialysis fluid by a semipermeable membrane. This allowed any toxic substances that had built up in the bloodstream, which would normally have been secreted by the kidneys, to diffuse out of the blood into the dialysis fluid."

Bockris goes on to note, "From this cure sprang the myth that Keith regularly had the blood emptied out of his body and replaced with a fresh supply. This Draculan notion is one of the few elements of his image that Richards has gone to some pains to correct, but to no avail."

In *Life*, Richards' own version of what actually went on in Switzerland is disappointingly sketchy. But then, heroin has a tendency to, let's say, blur the quotidian details of an addict's existence. In an earlier passage of the book, Richards noted that *that* was the best excuse for doing smack in the first place: Everything else kind of falls to the wayside.

Richards did manage to recall that he got massively loaded before making the trip to Switzerland. "Dope me up so I can sleep through as much of the seventy-two hours of hell as possible." The actual time the cure takes depends on whose version you read.

He also describes Dr. Denber as being American, though he "looked Swiss, close shaven and rimless glasses, Himmleresque. He spoke with a Midwestern twang."

Ultimately, all he says about the procedure is "In actual fact, Dr. Denber's treatment was useless for me. Dodgy little bugger, too. I'd have rather cleaned up with Smitty, Bill Burroughs's nurse, that hairy, old matron."

Richards eventually did kick heroin and claims he's been clean for thirty years. But the transfusion story persists, and you have to wonder at his continued denials, given that any tall tale told about him at this point only increases his legend. Heck, even the story of his falling out of a tree in Fiji and surviving brain surgery grew to mythic proportions. In spite of everything that's been thrown his way—including a good chunk of which he invited—he's rock's indefatigable, indestructible man, as steady and persistent as a 4/4 beat. ✖

CHAPTER 44

GENE SIMMONS' TONGUE BOVINE-ENHANCED?

A COW'S TONGUE IN THE KISS BASSIST'S MOUTH? DOESN'T SOUND KOSHER TO US . . .

KISS has long prided itself on big. Big show. Big costumes. Big hits. Big . . . appendages.

Biggest of the big, though, is the reputation enjoyed by bassist Gene Simmons' tongue.

The pink part of Simmons' anatomy that he can legally show is both a wonder and freak of nature. Flicked with great frequency during live shows, it's considerably longer than average and is displayed with a dexterity that certainly fires the imaginations of orally inclined members of the band's official fan club, the KISS Army.

And it's also all his own—despite reports to the contrary.

Early in KISS' career, while Simmons was still on his first photo album dedicated to Polaroids of groupies he allegedly pleasured, word spread—widely—that the enormous muscle was actually part cow tongue grafted onto Simmons' own. KISS' willingness to outrage certainly made that an amusing idea to consider, but it's not even close to the truth.

In his 2001 autobiography, *Kiss and Tell*, Simmons wrote with pride about realizing what a treasure he possessed within his mouth: "I was oblivious, for the first thirteen years of my life, that I was endowed with a large oral appendage, my superlong tongue. It really was longer than everyone else's, and I was soon to find out that having a long tongue came in handy with the girls." Asked about the bovine tongue rumor later on, he replied, "Nah. . . . Come on. Somebody's been spending too much time at the deli."

And actually, if one were to go to a deli—where beef tongue is a cold-cut staple on most menus—and took a gander at the raw material, it becomes clear how ludicrous the idea is.

Simmons, apparently, licks it all up without surgical aid. ✘

Gene Simmons, in all his lingual glory. *Paul Bergen/ Redferns/Getty Images*

Given the subject matter, "Lick It Up"—
the title track to the 1983 album that was
KISS' first sans makeup—seems like a perfect
soundtrack. Its insistent, chugging, eighth-note
rhythm is even a good speed for a little tongue-
flicking exercise.

MYTH TRACK

CHAPTER 45

DID ROD STEWART REALLY HAVE A STOMACH FULL OF . . . EWWWW!

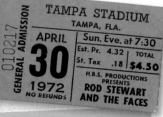

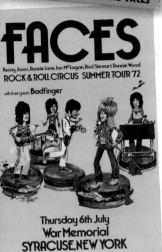

THAT'S PRETTY HARD TO SWALLOW.

"**S**ome guys have all the luck," Rod Stewart sang on his 1984 hit song of the same name. Rod the Mod certainly has had his share of good fortune since he began busking in London some fifty years ago—hit singles, multiplatinum record sales, frontman status in two key British bands (the Jeff Beck Group and the Faces), and a succession of girlfriends and wives that's included beauties such as Britt Ekland, Alana Stewart, Kelly Emberg, and Rachel Hunter.

He also has the dubious distinction for being the subject of one of pop culture's most enduring and readily accepted urban legends.

According to a story that began circulating in the late '70s or so, Stewart was partying it up while on tour in America—which city depends on the teller of the tale. He collapsed and was taken to a hospital. Faced with a rowdy rocker on the emergency room table, the doctor suspected a possible drug overdose and ordered Stewart's stomach pumped. Hospital personnel were shocked and scandalized to discover that the contents of his stomach included—and there's no delicate way to say it—a pint (heck, some say a gallon) of semen.

It's a tale that has been reported as fact ever since, by everyone from music journalists to radio DJs to record business executives to other musicians. Stewart addressed the myth, um, head-on, in a 1991 interview with *Rolling Stone*: "Oh, the Cum-in-the-Belly story?" he asked with a laugh. "That story spread all around the fucking world. What's amazing is that it's a story that never appeared in the press, as far as I know. I never read it or heard it anywhere on the radio. I wasn't even in the country at the time it supposedly happened. And you know I'm not a queer!"

The granddaddy of all rock myths? Rod Stewart sports a plaid and pleather ensemble, 1979. *Richard E. Aaron/Redferns/ Getty Images*

It should also be noted that no doctor or emergency room personnel, anywhere, stepped forward to offer proof that the incident did actually happen.

Writer Bill Zehme even tracked down urban folklorist and author Jan Harold Brunvand, who chalked up the Stewart story to a variation on a common myth known as "The Promiscuous Cheerleader" (in which a cheerleader services every member of one of her school's sports teams for winning the big game). Over the years the same fate has been prescribed to Stewart's good pal and fellow football (soccer) aficionado Elton John, Jon Bon Jovi, certain members of New Kids on the Block, and Justin Timberlake.

As for Stewart, he contended the rumor "was so laughable, it never really hurt me." Noting the substantial amount of semen said to be in his stomach, he added, "What could it have been? A fleet of fucking sailors? Or footballers? I mean, what the hell? Jesus Christ!" ✗

MYTH TRACK

It's not a song about his prodigious sexual exploits, though Rod has plenty of those, from "Maggie May" to "Tonight's the Night," "Hot Legs," "Da Ya Think I'm Sexy?," and on and on. But "Sailing," a song from his *Atlantic Crossing* album and Rod's biggest-selling single in the United Kingdom, is our choice here. The cover tune, written by Gavin Sutherland and first performed by the Sutherland Brothers Band, is indeed about sailing, which is done on boats, of course. And boats are full of what, exactly? If you said "seamen," you get the joke.

CHAPTER 46

MICHAEL'S MASTER MANIPULATIONS

THE HYPERBARIC CHAMBER, THE ELEPHANT MAN'S BONES, THE PLASTIC SURGERY— JUST HOW "WHACKO" WAS JACKO?

Michael Jackson's untimely death on June 25, 2009, has done much to massage public perception of the troubled singer, who in the preceding years was dogged by a fading career, collapsing finances, and allegations of child abuse that persisted despite a 2005 acquittal on all charges.

It may be asking too much of people today to consider two equal but opposing thoughts about any particular person. Our judgments, it seems, tend to be rendered, in a phrase pertinent to Jackson, black or white.

And so, the final word on Michael Jackson is that he was a singular performer—the King of Pop, as he wished to be called—and a child prodigy who grew up to become the *Guinness Book of World Records*–certified "Most Successful Performer of All Time." He was a musical superstar, a dance innovator, a fashion icon, and a trailblazer in the world of music video. His 1982 album *Thriller* is considered the best-selling album ever. He's a two-time inductee into the Rock and Roll Hall of Fame (with the Jackson 5 and as a solo artist), a member of the Dance Hall of Fame, and the recipient of hundreds of awards, including thirteen Grammys.

But let's face it: to put it mildly, the guy was also more than just a little eccentric—more than, to use one of his own album titles, off the wall.

And there was a time when that's exactly the way he wanted to be seen.

This was before the alleged child abuse or hush money. Before his bizarre (and brief) marriage to Lisa Marie Presley. Before his marriage to his dermatologist's assistant, Debbie Rowe, who bore him a son, Prince Michael, and a daughter, Paris Michael Katherine. Before the mysterious birth of another son, Prince Michael II (a.k.a. "Blanket"), who in 2002 Jackson infamously dangled off a fourth-floor hotel balcony in Berlin.

Before the allegations of child abuse and the baby-dangling, Jacko was seen simply as a singular performer—if mildly eccentric. *Ron Galella/ WireImage/Getty Images*

It was before Jackson tried to clear his name by having softballs lobbed at him in TV interviews with Diane Sawyer and Oprah Winfrey. Before albums such as *Dangerous*, *HIStory*, and *Invincible* were met with increasing indifference by the public. And before Martin Bashir's devastating *Living with Michael Jackson* television documentary spotlighted Jackson's deeply tattered psyche in ways previously unimaginable.

And it was before the singer abandoned his fabled Neverland Ranch, moved to the Middle East, and based his hopes for a triumphant comeback on a series of fifty concerts at London's O2 Arena, which never happened, of course, though the rehearsals were documented in the film *This Is It*.

Back when *Thriller* ruled the charts, however, the world was Jackson's oyster. His best buddies were Bubbles the Chimp and Elizabeth Taylor. He dated Diana Ross, Brooke Shields, and Jodie Foster, and was even feted at the White House by President Ronald Reagan.

During this period Jackson was seen as benignly eccentric. His face did seem to be changing, most likely due to plastic surgery, but what major star didn't avail him or herself of such conceits? More disturbingly, though, Jackson's skin appeared to be whitening and he began appearing in public wearing a thick coat of pancake makeup. Jackson explained that he suffered from vitiligo, a skin disorder that causes depigmentation, a claim confirmed in his autopsy. But rumors of skin bleaching persisted.

Such chatter kept Jackson's name in the press, though—a fact that didn't go unnoticed by the star himself. A disciple of P. T. Barnum, Jackson built much of his own myth by planting stories in the press, hoping to never leave the public's collective sight or mind.

Among the most famous such stories was the notion that he slept in a hyperbaric chamber. These tubelike devices, which flood body tissues with pure oxygen under increased barometric pressure, are used to treat victims of burns and decompression sickness. Jackson saw one at L.A.'s Brotman Medical Center, which housed the Michael Jackson Burn Unit that he established after being treated at the hospital for burns suffered in a notorious accident while filming a Pepsi commercial. After one of his doctors theorized that sleeping in a hyperbaric chamber could prolong life, Jackson looked into buying one but was dissuaded by his then-manager, Frank Dileo.

Still, Jackson asked to be photographed in the chamber, and in 1986 the photo was leaked to the *National Enquirer* in an elaborate cloak-and-dagger routine that involved Dileo and noted publicist Michael Levine. The photo was accompanied by a story suggesting that Jackson was using the chamber in an attempt to live to be 150 years old.

None of it was true, of course. But with multiple confirmations from Jackson's own camp, the *Enquirer* had no reason not to believe it. Nor did the numerous newspaper, magazine, television, and radio outlets that picked up the story and ran with it. Soon, the photo was seen all over the world.

For Jackson, the hoax was instructive. Not surprisingly, he was at it again a year later.

During a trip to England, Jackson was given special access to view the bones of Joseph Merrick (often incorrectly identified as John Merrick), a.k.a. the Elephant Man, a Victorian-age sideshow curiosity who suffered extreme physical deformities. Jackson was fascinated with Merrick, having seen David Lynch's 1980 film starring John Hurt. Jackson identified with Merrick's profound loneliness and outsider status.

The visit inspired Jackson's next stunt: making an offer to buy the Elephant Man's bones. Or at least telling the press he'd made an offer.

Again it worked, albeit this time a little too well, and when the press checked with the London Hospital Medical Center to verify the story, he had to put up or shut up. So in 1987 Jackson offered a million dollars for Merrick's remains. The hospital, sufficiently horrified, rejected the offer.

Jackson blamed the media for both stories, even though both were his own creation. The 1989 music video for his song "Leave Me Alone" featured sensational headlines about him in a tabloid called the *National Intruder*. Another sequence showed him performing alongside dancing Elephant Man–like bones. In 1993, he told Oprah, "I'm willing to forgive the press, or forgive anybody. I was taught to love and forgive, which I do have in my heart, but please don't believe these crazy, horrifying things."

The short-term effects of Jackson's adventures in self-mythology may have served their purpose. His tours sold out and *Thriller* continued to do boffo business, as did its 1987 follow-up, *Bad*. But it didn't take long for the press to turn on Jackson, especially the tabloids, which saw how well any item on Jackson—true or false—drove sales. They christened him "Wacko Jacko" and hounded him for every detail of his public and private life.

As that life spun—comically at first, but with ever-increasing tragedy—out of control, he did not disappoint them. ✗

The Grammy Award–winning video for "Leave Me Alone" may be the point where Jackson's success-driven ego tipped over into full-blown megalomania, celebrating himself while also lamenting how put-upon he was by the lying jackals of the media.

MYTH TRACK

CHAPTER 47

MARILYN MANSON'S SPARE RIB?

HOW BADLY DOES HE WANT TO HAVE SEX WITH HIMSELF? HE'S FLEXIBLE ON THE SUBJECT. ALSO, WAS HE PAUL ON *THE WONDER YEARS*?

Sell a few million records, declare yourself the Antichrist, and spend your days and nights exhibiting generally outrageous behavior, and you can expect that a few tales will be told at your expense.

That's been the experience of Brian Hugh Warner, a misfit kid from Canton, Ohio, and later Fort Lauderdale, Florida, who grew up to be latter-day shock rocker Marilyn Manson.

Myths about Manson abound. And given that his stage name juxtaposes those of film icon Marilyn Monroe and serial killer Charles Manson, and that his act has included the display of fascist-inspired banners, slashing himself with broken glass, tearing pages out of Bibles, wiping his nether regions with the American flag, and other assorted acts of premeditated mayhem, it's not surprising that he's managed to, let's say *lose control of the narrative*.

According to just a few stories, (a) Manson has passed puppies and chickens into the audience at his concerts and ordered them to be sacrificed before the show could begin; (b) at a Halloween show, Manson would commit suicide by blowing up the venue and everyone in it; (c) he's had his penis removed and breast implants inserted; (d) he's had his penis tattooed black; (e) he's had sex with animals onstage; (f) he and his band have sex onstage; (g) he pulls fans onstage, strips them naked, and has sex with them; and (h) he pulled a child onstage, sang happy birthday to him, and then had sex with him.

Marilyn Manson performs onstage in 2001, ribs and all. *TDC Photography/ Shutterstock.com*

And so on.

Those stories are all untrue, of course, having been cooked up by the overheated imagination of his own fans—who, let's face it, are an interesting and wholly self-selected group—or in affidavits distributed by various religious groups, most notably the American Family Association, which

MYTH TRACK

If the myth were true, how many ribs would Marilyn Manson have to remove to accomplish his goal? "It's all relative to the size of your steeple," is the obvious answer, a line from "The Beautiful People," the lead single from Manson's second full-length album, *Antichrist Superstar*. The track only made it to No. 26 on Billboard's Modern Rock chart, but is still considered one of Manson's signature tunes, thanks in large part to its oh-so-creepy video.

tries to have Manson's concerts postponed or even canceled, and sometimes succeed. Several such affidavits are quoted at length in Manson's 1998 autobiography, *The Long Hard Road Out of Hell*.

The one about the band members having sex may be partially true, given that on occasion, the sex toys that Manson has deployed during performances are mistaken by some for the real thing. As ever, though, outrage—like the definition of "is"—is in the eye of the beholder.

Two stories that have persisted, or at least top Manson's myth list, though, are that he had a rib (or two or three) surgically removed so he could perform autofellatio, and that, as a child, he played the character Paul on the TV series *The Wonder Years*. Variations on the latter item include that he didn't play Paul, but rather Winnie Cooper, on the show, and that he was a child actor on a different show, *Mr. Belvedere*.

Paul was actually played by actor Josh Saviano, whose visage bears a passing resemblance to the preteen Brian Warner. No doubt the myth was made more tantalizing by the fact that Saviano dropped out of Hollywood and could easily have emerged anywhere—even as a polymorphously perverse, drug-celebrating, makeup-smeared rocker who happens to be a card-carrying minister in the Church of Satan. As it happened, though, Saviano decided to leave acting for academia. He majored in political science at Yale and graduated from Yeshiva's Benjamin N. Cardozo School of Law in Manhattan. Today's he's an attorney practicing in New York.

Of the case of mistaken identity, Saviano is loath to deny it, telling *People* magazine, "What would you rather have, people thinking you're a dorky kid from *The Wonder Years* or a satanic rock star? It's way cooler."

The Winnie Cooper variation is obviously inspired by the feminine stage name chosen by Manson as well as his cross-dressing ways. But that role was played by Danica McKellar, who continued to act (most notably in shows like *The West Wing* and *Inspector Mom*), but also made her mark in mathematics, graduating *summa cum laude* from UCLA. She also helped prove a new math theorem (dubbed the Chayes-McKellar-Winn theorem) and has written books intended to inspire young girls to pursue mathematics.

The child actor who played perpetually awkward teenager Kevin Owens in *Mr. Belvedere* is Rob Stone. He's done some acting since then and later went on to direct documentary films, including the CableAce Award–winning *Blue Angels: Around the World at the Speed of Sound*.

The rib removal/autofellatio story is more intriguing, not merely for being more exotic, but because such pursuits seem in line with Manson's interests. In his book, he admits that scarification and body modification are among his "hobbies," and he spills a lot of ink cataloging his sexual exploits as well.

But really, this is just a variation on the myth that other celebrities—usually actresses, including Elizabeth Taylor and Jane Fonda—had their lower ribs removed. Not for sexual self-gratification, mind you, but rather to retain their svelte figures and remain, as Manson might put it, among "The Beautiful People."

Tempting though it is to believe, it wasn't true in those cases, either.

Manson brought several of these themes together in an undated journal entry published in *The Long Hard Road Out of Hell*: "If I'd really gotten my ribs removed, I would have been busy sucking my own dick on *The Wonder Years* instead of chasing Winnie Cooper," he wrote. "Besides, I wouldn't have sucked other people's dicks onstage, either. I would have been sucking my own. Plus, who really has time to be killing puppies when you can be sucking your own dick? I think I'm gonna call a surgeon in the morning." **X**

A BONE OF THEIR OWN

OTHER MUSICAL ARTISTS—all of them women—have been accused of having their lower ribs removed, but not for the purposes of self-gratification, á la Monsieur Manson. Instead, they did it, it was whispered, to keep their midriffs as trim as possible for maximum sex appeal.

Jane Fonda, Elizabeth Taylor, Pamela Anderson, and Kate Moss have battled rib-removal rumors in the past. In the world of music, the finger is pointed at artists like Janet Jackson, Britney Spears, Shakira, and, most often, Cher, whose perennially svelte figure makes her suspect in the eyes of some.

Cher admits she's had several procedures to maintain her looks, notably a nose job, a breast augmentation, braces on her teeth, and, of course, many tattoos. But in 1988, when *Paris Match* magazine made the claim that Cher had ribs removed, she sued the publication and won.

By way of further denying the myth, it should be pointed out that Cher is a workout fanatic who published *Cher Forever Fit: The Lifetime Plan for Fitness, Health & Beauty* in 1991 and released a couple of workout videos soon after. She has also rightly pointed out that the revealing costumes she is known for wearing wouldn't make too many allowances for the scars that a rib-removal procedure would likely leave.

So while she may not have had any ribs taken out, Cher did suffer one disastrous operation, having her critical reputation excised when, after winning a Best Actress Oscar for *Moonstruck*, she started doing infomercials.

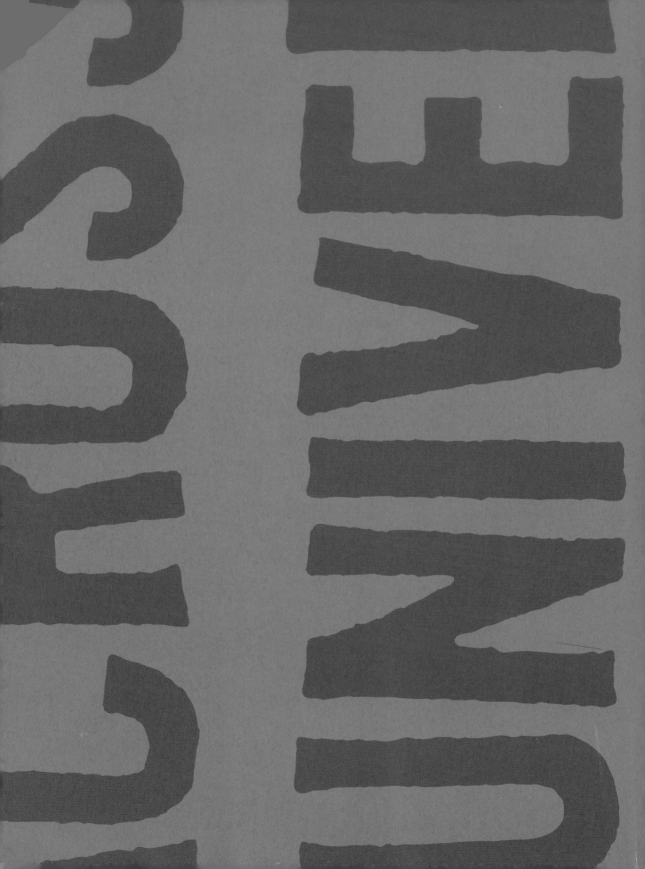

ACROSS THE
UNIVERSE

CHAPTER 48

HOW MUCH TIME DID JOHNNY CASH REALLY DO?

THE MAN IN BLACK NEVER WENT TO PRISON— STILL, IT WAS SOMETHING TO SING ABOUT.

Johnny and June Carter leave the Kansas State Penitentiary in 1968. Cash was there voluntarily—not as an inmate. *Hulton Archive/Getty Images*

Maybe it's because Johnny Cash sang so often and so convincingly about prison—or that two of his most famous albums, *At Folsom Prison* and *At San Quentin*, were recorded behind stone walls and guarded gates— that people think Cash did hard time himself.

Not so.

"A lot of people will jump on anything to try and bring an artist down," Cash said. "Everybody knows I didn't shoot a man in Reno just to watch him die, but a lot of people like to hear that. It's a fun thing with me."

Certainly Cash cut a mythical figure throughout his long and storied career, if only for his ability to embody seemingly irreconcilable positions in so many areas of his life. He was a deeply religious man, yet his reputation as a rock 'n' roll hellion stood second to none. He was a recovering drug addict who was saved by the Bible and the love of a woman—his wife, June Carter Cash—but whose weaknesses occasionally led him back to rehab. He was a dyed-in-the-wool patriot whose bitter criticism of the Vietnam War flew in the face of country music's traditionally hard-line conservatism. And heck, his best friends were fellow troublemaker Waylon Jennings and the Reverend Billy Graham—no small feat, that.

In short, Cash was a man who truly inhabited the line Kris Kristofferson wrote about him in "He's a Pilgrim": "He's a walking contradiction partly truth and partly fiction."

Johnny Cash, booked on drug possession in El Paso, Texas, 1965. *Michael Ochs Archives/Getty Images*

Then, too, Cash was the fabled "Man in Black," so called for the famously monochromatic wardrobe that he donned—as he wrote in his self-defining hit of the same name—for the poor, the oppressed, the sick, and those who have not been transformed by the word of God.

And yet, rumors dogged him that he himself had been a guest at the Graybar Hotel.

But no wonder. Cash's self-destructive ways, especially during the early '60s, left plenty of victims besides him in their wake. He canceled concerts, bankrupting some of the small-time promoters who had stretched their lines of credit to book him. Friendships both professional and personal were shattered by his irresponsibility. He crashed almost every car he owned, crazed by the manic energy of his addictions, and once drove a tractor into a lake, escaping only because he was thrown off on the way down.

Cash even started a forest fire, burning hundreds of acres of California's Los Padres National Forest when an overheated wheel bearing in the truck he was driving caused the vehicle to ignite. He claimed he was the only person to be sued by the government for starting a forest fire.

But still, Cash served no prison time. He *did* spend some time behind bars, though, but only for single-night stays—seven by his own count. The charges were all for misdemeanors ranging from drug possession—cops thought he was smuggling heroin, but he actually was carrying a quantity of prescription pills—to picking flowers on private property (see "Starkville City Jail" on *San Quentin*).

What finally pulled Cash out of his self-destructive life was a sobering experience following an arrest for a car crash and possession of still more prescription drugs. "There was a sheriff named Ralph Jones," Cash explained. "He let me out of jail one morning in LaFayette, Georgia, and gave me my pills back that he had taken from me the night before. He said, 'God has given you free will. Here's your pills. Go ahead and kill yourself. That's what you were doing when you came in here.' But this is what got me: He said, 'I told my wife when I got home that I had Johnny Cash in my jail, and she cried all night. She's such a fan of yours and loves you so much.' He said, 'I don't want to see you no more.'

"I went right straight back to Nashville and called June, and she contacted Dr. Nat Winston, who was the former head of the Tennessee Department for Mental Health. He came out to my house every day for 30 days. There weren't any treatment centers around back then. I climbed the walls and beat the devil there for a while. And I came out clean and straight." **X**

MYTH TRACK

From the beginning of his career, Johnny Cash wrote convincingly about prison life, even if he never spent a day in stir himself. Cash adapted one of his earliest hits, "Folsom Prison Blues," from composer Gordon Jenkins' "Crescent City Blues." This was after Cash saw the 1951 film *Inside the Walls of Folsom Prison* while serving in the air force, stationed in West Germany. "Folsom Prison Blues" became a Top 5 country hit and one of Cash's signature songs, in no small part due to the infamous line "I shot a man in Reno just to watch him die," perhaps the most gangsta moment in country music history.

CHAPTER 49

DID CHARLES MANSON EVER MONKEE AROUND?

BUDDING MURDERER AUDITIONED FOR *THE* PREFAB FOUR? YOU'RE KILLIN' US!

In 1965, the production company Screen Gems put out a casting call for "Folk & Rock Musicians-Singers" and "4 Insane Boys, aged 17–21" for "acting roles" in a then-unspecified TV series. They got responses from some notable hopefuls, including a pre–Buffalo Springfield Stephen Stills, future Three Dog Night member Danny Hutton, and songwriters Paul Williams and Harry Nilsson.

According to legend, convicted mass murderer Charles Manson was also among the 437 aspirants who turned up to audition for what would become *The Monkees* TV series—a great story, but not a true one.

In actuality, Manson was in prison at the time the auditions were held. He was at Terminal Island in San Pedro, California, for violating his probation on a 1958 conviction for forging a U.S. Treasury check. Manson, who was indicted on a Mann Act violation in 1960, was granted parole on March 21, 1967, by which time *The Monkees* was on the air and the group was all over the pop charts.

Even if he had shown up to the audition, Manson would have been thirty years old—well beyond the producers' parameters.

The Monkees' own Micky Dolenz is willing to take credit for starting this particular myth. "I was doing a radio show in L.A., and the interviewer said something like, 'Well, I heard a lot of people auditioned for the Monkees,'" Dolenz recalls. "And I said something like, 'Yeah, including Charlie Manson, ha, ha, ha,' and somebody picked up on that. Things turn into urban legend pretty quickly. But there's no record of him showing up for the audition."

Manson did, however, pursue some musical interests as both a songwriter and performer after getting out of jail in 1967. He befriended Beach Boys drummer Dennis Wilson and lived for a time in Wilson's home. Wilson, in turn, introduced Manson to Columbia Records executive Terry Melcher (the

In the end, Charles Manson was more suited for prison bars than these monkey bars. *Keystone Features/ Getty Images*

son of screen and TV star Doris Day) and funded recording sessions for Manson. Wilson also allegedly rewrote a Manson song called "Cease to Exist," re-titled it "Never Learn Not to Love," and took sole credit for it when it was released as the B-side of the Beach Boys' single "Bluebirds Over the Mountain" and on the group's 1969 album, *20/20*. That same summer, of course, Manson and members of his "Family" murdered seven people in the Los Angeles area, and he's now serving a life sentence at California's Corcoran State Prison.

The Monkees' audition ad, meanwhile, netted only one member for the group: Michael Nesmith. Dolenz, already the star of the NBC children's show *Circus Boy*, was referred by his agent. Davy Jones was under contract to Screen Gems, and Peter Tork was referred by Stills, his roommate at the time. The show was phenomenally successful, with fifty-eight episodes airing from September 1966 to September 1968, while the group sold 50 million albums worldwide and notched twelve Top 40 singles. Nilsson ("Cuddly Toy") and Williams ("Someday Man") were counted among a Monkees songwriting corps that also included Carole King and Neil Diamond—but not Manson. ✘

MYTH TRACK

Just because he didn't audition for the Monkees doesn't mean that Charles Manson never had a recording career. With the help of Phil Kaufman, who had met Manson while both were in prison (and who elsewhere in this book can be found stealing and burning the corpse of Gram Parsons), Manson released the album *Lie: The Love & Terror Cult* in 1970. Recorded in 1968 and '69, the album contains "Look at Your Game Girl," a song later covered, controversially, by Guns N' Roses. The original sounds nothing like the ravings of a maniac whose murderous rampage was designed to spark a race war, but rather like any other lovelorn plaint written by a wannabe rock star in the late '60s.

CHAPTER 50

WAS A FUTURE SNL ALUM IN STEELY DAN?

HE'S CHEVY CHASE, AND YOU'RE NOT . . . GOING TO CONTINUE BELIEVING HE WAS THE DRUMMER IN STEELY DAN.

"**M**embership" is a loose term when it comes to Steely Dan.

Though it began as a sextet in 1972, the group is essentially a duo—Donald Fagen and Walter Becker—who have employed scores of studio hands while crafting some of the most intricately arranged and produced music to ever grace the pop charts, bridging the jazz/rock divide on albums such as *The Royal Scam* and *Aja*. But despite reports to the contrary, actor Chevy Chase was never one of those members.

He did, however, play music with Fagen and Becker—at Bard College in Annandale-on-Hudson, New York.

Despite more academic leanings—he was pre-med at Bard, earning a bachelor of arts degree in English—Cornelius Crane Chase came to school with perfect pitch and some accomplishment playing drums and keyboards. Fagen, meanwhile, was what Becker called "the dean of the pick-up band syndrome," or as Steely Dan biographer Brian Sweet noted, "the piano-playing jack-of-all-trades who could at short notice assemble whichever type of group was needed for whatever kind of dance or party," including ensembles such as the Bad Rock Group, the Don Fagen Jazz Trio, and the Leather Canary, the latter of which featured Chase on drums.

Chase described the Leather Canary as "a bad jazz band" not long before he graduated from Bard in 1967. Classified 4-F by the draft board—he claimed, untruthfully, that he had "homosexual tendencies"—Chase decided to eschew medical school and instead focus on entertainment. He played in a rock band called Chamaeleon Church, which recorded an album and broke up in 1969. He wrote for *National Lampoon* magazine and TV's *The Smothers Brothers Comedy Hour* before becoming part of *The National Lampoon Radio Hour*, which led to his fame-making

Steely Dan may not have had Chevy Chase behind the kit, but they still became major dudes in their own right. *Michael Ochs Archives/Getty Images*

casting on *NBC's Saturday Night* (later renamed *Saturday Night Live*) and a subsequent career as an actor in films such as *Caddyshack*, *National Lampoon's Vacation*, *National Lampoon's Christmas Vacation*, *Fletch*, and more.

Fagen and Becker, meanwhile, took their musical show on the road after leaving Bard in 1969 (when Fagen graduated), first to the Brill Building as songwriters—their big break was "I Mean to Shine" for Barbra Streisand in 1971—then on tour as part of an incarnation of Jay & the Americans. ABC Records staff producer Gary Katz invited the duo to move to Los Angeles as staff writers for the label, and after they struck out on that front, Katz suggested Fagen and Becker form their own band, which they did with Jim Hodder as the original drummer.

The rest is, as they say, musical history. Steely Dan—named after a six-foot chrome dildo in William S. Burroughs' *Naked Lunch* (total truth, no myth there)—has sold more than 30 million copies of its nine studio albums; scored hit singles such as "Do It Again," "Reelin' in the Years," "Peg," "FM," and more; and was inducted into the Rock and Roll Hall of Fame in 2001. ✖

MYTH TRACK

No recorded evidence exists of the days Chevy Chase spent drumming in the Leather Canary with Donald Fagen and Walter Becker. But "My Old School" from Steely Dan's 1973 sophomore album, *Countdown to Ecstasy*, fits the bill since the Leather Canary played together at Bard College, Fagen, Becker, and Chase's old school.

WHAT WAS BOB DYLAN'S MOTORCYCLE NIGHTMARE?

DID A MOTORCYCLE ACCIDENT NEARLY KILL HIM . . . OR SAVE HIS LIFE?

During a December 1965 press conference in San Francisco, televised on Bay Area public station KQED, Bob Dylan turned the typical artist/reporter thrust-and-parry that's taken place throughout his career into absurdist theater, firing questions back at his inquisitors or answering with puzzling one-liners.

Early on in the event, Dylan was asked about the image of motorcycles in his songwriting. "Oh, we all like motorcycles to some degree" was as much as he would allow.

Dylan did like motorcycles, though, and it was only seven months after that press conference that a mishap on a motorcycle nearly took his life. Or saved it, depending on whom you believe.

The details of the cause and severity of the crash are hazy, and Dylan has told a variety of differing accounts over the years. In one version, he hit an oil slick on a road near his home in Woodstock, New York, and went flying over the handlebars; in another, he was blinded by the sun and accidentally locked up the brakes. Some early reports said that Dylan was dead or horribly disfigured, possibly paralyzed. Dylan himself said that he'd fractured several vertebrae and suffered a concussion. Still other accounts said the accident was a complete fiction that Dylan used as cover for going into hiding.

There's considerable evidence for the latter theory. No ambulance was called to the scene of the accident, and Dylan wasn't hospitalized—rather lax treatment for a broken neck by anyone's standards. Then, too, Dylan had just returned from a grueling European tour during which his loud, electrified music was pilloried by critics and booed by sellout crowds of folk purists. Former fans called him "traitor," "Judas," and worse.

Bob Dylan and his ill-fated Triumph motorcycle.
Douglas R. Gilbert/ Redferns/Getty Images

Dylan reportedly emerged from his motorcycle accident a more reflective person. He made his famous Isle of Wight Festival appearance on August 31, 1969, a few months after releasing *Nashville Skyline*. *Anwar Hussein/Getty Images*

Sixty additional concerts had been scheduled for the coming months, and Dylan owed the finished manuscript of his poetry book, *Tarantula*, to publisher Macmillan as well as footage for a possible TV show to the ABC network.

It was as good a time as any to get off the merry-go-round.

"I'd just about had it . . . . I'd had it with the whole scene, whether I knew it or didn't know it," Dylan admitted in Martin Scorsese's 2005 documentary film *Bob Dylan: No Direction Home*. "I was ready to quit for a while. . . . Just being pressed and hammered and expected to answer questions is enough to make anybody sick, really."

Still, it's likely that *something* physically debilitating happened to Dylan, perhaps even the reputed motorcycle accident. In his biography *No Direction Home: The Life and Music of Bob Dylan*, Robert Shelton quotes various sources who saw Dylan around that time saying he was having difficulty with his eyes and couldn't work, or that he was wearing a brace. Filmmaker D. A. Pennebaker said, "I knew he'd been hurt in other ways, so in either event, what he was doing was recovering."

Asked about the accident in subsequent interviews, Dylan has almost always been circumspect. In 1969, he spoke to *Rolling Stone*'s Jann Wenner about the span between his albums *Blonde on Blonde* and *John Wesley Harding*: "At that time I had a dreadful motorcycle accident . . . which put me away for a while . . . and I still didn't sense the importance of that accident till at least a year after that. I realized that it was a *real* accident. I mean I thought that I was just gonna get up and go back to doing what I was doing before . . . but I couldn't do it anymore."

Wenner asked him what changes the accident wrought. "What change?" Dylan said. "Well, it . . . it limited me. It's hard to speak about the change, you know? It's not the type of change that one can put into words . . . besides the physical change. I had a busted vertebrae; neck vertebrae. And there's really not much to talk about. I don't want to talk about it."

Regardless of the mystery, what's clear is that the time off allowed Dylan to clear his head, rid himself of toxic relationships, and possibly toxic substances as well. Some accounts have him using the time off to kick an amphetamine habit, or perhaps even heroin.

Left alone in his bucolic upstate New York surroundings (except for the occasional reporter or fan on a quest—this was decades prior to the constant celebrity hounding of Perez Hilton and TMZ), Dylan's creativity came back to the fore. He wrote and recorded a flood of material with his backing band, the Hawks (later the Band), in their nearby house, known as Big Pink. The tracks surfaced on much-sought-after bootlegs and only years later were officially released as *The Basement Tapes*.

Dylan's next album was *John Wesley Harding*, a low-key, acoustic affair that lyrically reflected his period of solitude and deep thought. He appeared again onstage on January 20, 1968, at a concert paying tribute to his recently deceased hero, Woody Guthrie. But Dylan wouldn't tour again until 1974, with the Band in tow.

In his 2004 memoir, *Chronicles*, Dylan summed up his days in the wilderness succinctly: "I had been in a motorcycle accident and I'd been hurt, but I recovered. Truth was that I wanted to get out of the rat race." **X**

MYTH TRACK

Dylan didn't record the single "Watching the River Flow" (later collected on his *Greatest Hits Vol. 2*) until nearly five years after his reputed motorcycle accident and subsequent hibernation in Woodstock, New York. But the song captures his feeling of deep contentment at simply lying back and biding his time. Elsewhere, people are being disagreeable, hassling each other, and breaking down emotionally in the middle of the street, but as Dylan sings, "This ol' river keeps on rollin', though/No matter what gets in the way and which way the wind does blow."

52 WAS GRACE SLICK'S DAUGHTER NAMED ON IMPULSE, OR WAS IT PREPLANNED?

JEFFERSON AIRPLANE FRONTWOMAN CREATED "GOD" IN HER OWN IMAGE.

Fans, to say nothing of overbearing hospital staffers, don't say much these days when celebrities name their offspring something unusual—like Heavenly Hiraani Tiger Lily, daughter of INXS's Michael Hutchence and TV host Paula Yates, or Hud and Speck, sons of John Mellencamp and model Elaine Irwin.

That wasn't always the case, however. On January 25, 1971, Jefferson Airplane principals Grace Slick and Paul Kantner welcomed a daughter into the world at French Hospital in San Francisco. Ironically, Slick—a champion of drug use, who, in the psychedelic anthem "White Rabbit," advised listeners to "feed your head"—wound up practicing natural childbirth because the anesthetist never showed up.

In her autobiography *Somebody to Love?*, the singer recalled that, after she gave birth, a Spanish nurse came into her room with a certificate to sign. "She said, 'We give these to all the new mothers,'" Slick wrote. "'You see, it says where she was born, what time, and the name of the baby goes here.' She pointed to an empty line in the document. 'What is your baby's name?' she asked.

"I noticed a crucifix around her neck and spontaneously said, 'god. We spell it with a small g because we want her to be humble.' It was only a few hours after my baby had arrived, I was holding the miracle of birth in my arms, and I was already messing with somebody's head."

Grace Slick with her newborn daughter, god. Clearly, she never heard "A Boy Named Sue."
AP Photo/Bob Klein

Slick says the nurse, "deciding that the blasphemy was real," dutifully wrote the name on the certificate, "probably expecting to go through her life repeating novenas for her participation in this profanity."

Then, Slick claims, the nurse called *San Francisco Chronicle* columnist Herb Caen, who published the baby's name, leading to predictable outrage.

Slick presented the naming of the child as spontaneous, but a *Rolling Stone* interview from earlier in the year suggests otherwise. She told writer Ben Fong-Torres that she and Kantner were going to call the baby god. "Just god," said Grace. "No last name, no capital G. And he can change his name when he feels like it."

Somehow, the infant wound up with the name China instead. "San Francisco has a large Asian community," Slick explained in her book, "and Paul and I observed that the Chinese follow spiritual practices that seem to offer more equanimity than the fear- and guilt-ridden dogmas of the Judeo-Christian ethic. Thousands of years before the Western Bible was written and rewritten and burned, and rewritten again during the Inquisition, the Oriental people had realized that the yin/yang or 50/50 take on human existence produces more acceptance and self-control. To Paul and me, this seemed a better alternative to the 'damned if you do, damned if you don't' ethic that permeates Western civilization."

A FEW MORE MUSICIANS AND THEIR STRANGELY NAMED PROGENY

Chris Martin and Gwyneth Paltrow: Apple
Donovan and Linda Lawrence: Astrella Celeste and Oriole Nebula
U2's The Edge (Dave Evans) and Aislinn O'Sullivan: Blue Angel
Alice and Sheryl Cooper: Calico, Dash, and Sonora Rose
Geri Halliwell: Bluebell Madonna
Bob Geldof and Paula Yates: Fifi Trixibell, Peaches, and Pixie
Sting and Frances Tomelty: Fuschsia
Jermaine Jackson and Alejandra Genevieve Oaziaza: Jermajesty
Sonny Bono and Cher: Chastity (now Chas)
Bono (Paul Hewson) and Ali Hewson: Memphis Eve
Andre Benjamin (Andre 3000) and Erykah Badu: Seven Sirius
Mariah Carey and Nick Cannon: Monroe and Moroccan
Michael Jackson and ?: Prince Michael II (a.k.a. Blanket)

Whew—never mind the god thing. That's a pretty heavy trip to lay on the kid right there.

But Slick and Kantner weren't alone. On the way to giving their children unusual names, other musicians have hit a few dips in the road, most notably Frank Zappa and his wife, Gail. They were already the parents of Moon Unit (whose name would have been Motorhead had she been a boy) when they welcomed a son into the family.

Filling out the paperwork at Hollywood Presbyterian Hospital, the couple ran into a nurse even more judgmental about names than Slick's turned out to be.

The name they had chosen for their child was "Dweezil," which was Frank's nickname for his wife's little toe.

"The nurse pleaded and pleaded with us not to name the child Dweezil," Zappa wrote in *The Real Frank Zappa Book*. "Labor pains and all, she was going to make Gail stand there unless we gave her another name to put on the form. I couldn't see letting Gail suffer just to argue to point, so I rattled off an assortment of first names of guys we knew: **Ian** (Underwood), **Donald (Van Vliet)**, **Calvin** (Schenkel), **Euclid** (James "Motorhead" Sherwood). As a result, Dweezil's original birth certificate name was **Ian Donald Calvin Euclid Zappa**. The nurse thought that was okay."

Moon and Dweezil were later joined by a brother, Ahmet Emuukha Rodan, and a sister, Diva Thin Muffin Pigeen.

"People make a lot of fuss about my kids having such supposedly 'strange names,'" Zappa wrote, 'but the fact is that no matter what first names I might have given them, it's **the last name** that is going to get them in trouble." ✘

MYTH TRACK

In his Shel Silverstein–penned novelty hit, "A Boy Named Sue," Johnny Cash tells the story of a child hell-bent on revenge against a father who gave him an unusual name—unusual for a boy, anyway. He tracks the old man down and they fight, after which the father explains himself and the son begins to see things his way. In the end, he reflects, "If I ever have a son, I think I'm gonna name him . . . *Bill or George, anything but Sue*!" Listen to the song and learn the lesson, people.

CHAPTER 53

HOW DID VINCE BECOME ALICE?

WAS IT THE RESULT OF A OUIJA BOARD SESSION? OOPS, WRONG CHANNEL . . .

I n 1968, a fledgling rock band in Los Angeles called the Nazz discovered that there was another band with the same name—based in Philadelphia and led by Todd Rundgren, and enjoying a national hit with "Open My Eyes."

Back to the drawing board.

The L.A. quintet, which had formed during the mid-'60s in Phoenix, Arizona, had already been through a few names, including the Earwigs and the Spiders. This time, however, they lit on something more provocative: Alice Cooper.

The story told at the time, and for many years hence, was that singer Vincent Furnier, who would go on to adopt the Alice name as his own, channeled the new moniker during a Ouija board session with the group's tour manager and his sister and their mother. Alice Cooper was supposedly a sixteenth-century English witch who presented herself to Furnier, who in turn felt enough of a kindred spirit to take the name.

Guitarist Michael Bruce later wrote in his 1996 memoir, *No More Mr. Nice Guy: The Inside Story of the Alice Cooper Group*, that the witch part was actually "embellished" and appended to the band name by a staffer at the Cheetah Club in Los Angeles.

But the Ouija board story persisted until Cooper published his 2007 autobiography, *Alice Cooper, Golf Monster*. In it, he wrote that the name came from a band meeting, where the group members resolved to come

The name of the band is probably the least questionable thing in this photo. *Michael Ochs Archives/Getty Images*

up with "something spooky" because their act had become more theatrical and even macabre. "The first name out of my mouth was a girl's name, Alice Cooper. Alice. Cooper. By the end of the night, the name kind of stuck. There was something about it. I conjured up the image of a little girl with a lollipop in one hand and a butcher knife in the other. Lizzie Borden. Alice Cooper. They had a similar ring."

Furnier embraced Alice Cooper as a character at first—he'd legally change his name in 1974—taking "her" look from Bette Davis' performance in *Whatever Happened to Baby Jane?*, a favorite film of the band members. "In the movie, Bette wears disgusting caked makeup smeared on her face . . . with deep, dark eyeliner. She looks horrific and creepy because she put on traditional makeup thickly and badly," Cooper wrote. He added that he was also influenced by the Great Tyrant, a character played by Anita Pallenberg (a longtime love of the Rolling Stones' Keith Richards) in *Barbarella*, who "dressed in black leather with a black eye patch and had switchblades coming out of her."

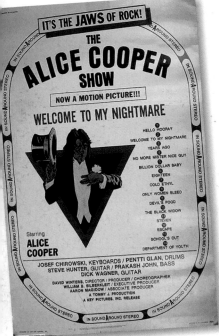

"Alice Cooper's look evolved from a composite of those female movie characters, with a little bit of Emma Peel from *The Avengers* added for good measure," Cooper explained. "Not bad. The name is Alice Cooper. A guy, not a girl. A group, not a solo act. A villain, not a hero or an idol. A woman killer. Weird. Eerie. Twisted. Ambiguous. It all came together—and nobody was doing anything remotely similar. On top of it all, everyone in the band was straight."

The name certainly caught people's imagination—attracting some, repelling others, and sometimes repelling those it attracted. The Alice Cooper group was renowned on the L.A. scene for driving people out of its shows. Even future manager Shep Gordon told author Bob Greene that when he first saw the band, "I saw people streaming out of a club as soon as the band began to play, and knew that I had a winner. . . . I had never seen such a strong

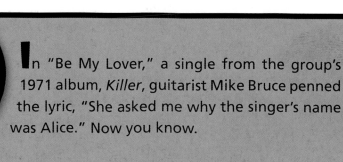

In "Be My Lover," a single from the group's 1971 album, *Killer*, guitarist Mike Bruce penned the lyric, "She asked me why the singer's name was Alice." Now you know.

negative reaction. People *hated* Alice, and I knew that anyone who could generate such strong negative energy had the potential to be a star, if the handling of the situation worked."

That it did. Mixing theatrics, controversy, and publicity stunts—not to mention some pretty decent records—the group ran off a string of four platinum and one gold album between 1971 and 1975, and Cooper (the man) has remained a rock 'n' roll icon since the group broke up in 1975. He isn't always Alice, though; some have called him Coop, his family calls him Vince, crewmembers have called him Vinnie and Boss. His wife, Sheryl, however, calls him Alice—and his three kids "are always explaining why their dad has such a funny name." ✖

OTHER SHOCK ROCKERS WHO HAVE ADOPTED SINISTER ALIASES

Zackary Baker = Zacky Vengeance (Avenged Sevenfold)
Dave Brokie = Oderus Urungus (Gwar)
Robert Cummings = Rob Zombie
Michael Cummings = Spider One (Powerman 5000)
Robert Deal = Mick Mars (Mötley Crüe)
Frank Feranna Jr. = Nikki Sixx (Mötley Crüe)
Brian Haner Jr. = Synyster Gates (Avenged Sevenfold)
Jack Kilcoyne = Pig Benis (Mushroomhead)
Kim Petersen = King Diamond (Mercyful Fate)
Tomi Putaansuu = Mr. Lordi (Lordi)
Matthew Sanders = M. Shadows (Avenged Sevenfold)
Brian Warner = Marilyn Manson

54

WAS PINK FLOYD OFF TO SEE THE WIZARD?

THE DARK SIDE OF THE MOON AND THE WIZARD OF OZ—A MARRIAGE MADE IN . . . AN ALTERNATE REALITY.

The members of Pink Floyd certainly had grand ambitions in 1972 when they set out to make what would be their landmark album, *The Dark Side of the Moon*. What they weren't doing, however, was creating a new soundtrack for *The Wizard of Oz*—at least on any level of consciousness.

Nevertheless, during the early '90s word began to spread in the underground that there was an incredible synchronicity between the album and the equally iconic film. Fans swore that if the two were cued up properly—and the album was played twice through—there were more than a hundred moments where *The Dark Side*'s music was perfectly synced to what was happening onscreen, the most commonly cited being the Scarecrow beginning to dance during the song "Brain Damage."

But any connection was purely coincidental, according to the Floyd camp. "It was hard enough just making the album, let alone making it work with a film," guitarist David Gilmour said with a laugh. "I think whoever supposedly figured that out has a little too much time on his hands."

Drummer Nick Mason, meanwhile, cracked, "Oh yes, we actually had Judy Garland in the studio," before deeming the claims bogus, too. "It is remarkable; you immediately start thinking, 'Who on earth spends that much time fitting it together?'" Mason did, however, acknowledge, "I've seen some of it. It is remarkable, but I think also it's worth bearing in mind that the brain is absolutely brilliant at knitting together any piece of music with any visual cue. I assume there are people out there now trying to fit *The Wall* to *Gladiator* or I don't know what else. The mind boggles at how much time must be wasted with people sitting there with albums trying to make them fit to movies."

Pink Floyd in 1968, four years before *The Dark Side of the Moon*. Though the *Oz* theory is bunk, according to drummer Nick Mason, the album *would* lead the band to an emerald city—one made out of stacks of money. *Michael Ochs Archive/Getty Images*

Alan Parsons, who engineered *The Dark Side*, later told *Rolling Stone* magazine that any discussion of a deliberate link between the album and film is "such a non-starter, a complete load of eyewash. I tried it for the first time about two years ago. . . . I was very disappointed. The only thing I noticed was that the line 'balanced on the biggest wave' came up when Dorothy was kind of tightrope walking along a fence." Parsons added that, "One of the things any audio professional will tell you is that the scope for the drift between the video and the record is enormous; it could be anything up to 20 seconds by the time the record's finished. And anyway, if you play any record with the sound turned down on the TV, you will find things that work."

The *Dark Side/Oz* proponents certainly did. While the connection was purported mostly via the still-nascent Internet during the early '90s, it received mainstream coverage starting in about 1995, shortly after Pink Floyd's last world tour; in fact, *Oz*-associated images—a girl with ruby slippers and a bicycle with a basket—on the cover of *Pulse*, the live album from that tour, gave even more credence to the claims. Websites popped up devoted to the supposed synchronicity, and clubs and theaters began screening *Oz* while playing *The Dark Side* alongside it. Turner Classic Movies did the same on air in July 2000. The Flaming Lips performed their version of the album in concert accompanied by *The Wizard of Oz* footage.

The project even had its own names, including *Dark Side of the Rainbow*, *Dark Side of Oz*, and *The Wizard of Floyd*.

Pink Floyd's members weren't the only ones to poke fun at the connection. The TV shows *Family Guy*, *The Colbert Report*, *How I Met Your Mother*, and *Raising Hope* have all referenced it, and in the 2005 film *The Muppets' Wizard of Oz*, the character Pepe the King Prawn says in an aside to the audience, "Those of you who have *Dark Side of the Moon*, press play now." In the commentary track of the DVD for *Tenacious D in the Pick of Destiny*, Jack Black comments, "If you start playing *Dark Side of the Moon* at this point in the film . . . it doesn't sound very good at all."

And in its song "Come Downstairs & Say Hello," the band Guster sings "Dorothy moves to click her ruby shoes/Right in tune with *Dark Side of the Moon*."

The Dark Side has hardly suffered for the association, of course. The 1973 release remains one of the best-selling albums of all time, with nearly 25 million copies in the United States and another 4 million-plus in Pink Floyd's native Great Britain. It set a record for spending 741 weeks on the Billboard 200 chart and has been on the trade magazine's Top Pop Catalogs Album chart since it began in May 1991. ✘

"And you are young and life is long, and there is time to kill today . . ." Dorothy rests in the field of poppies. *Silver Screen Collection/ Getty Images*

MYTH TRACK

Pink Floyd may call cash "a crime" in *The Dark Side of the Moon*'s hit single "Money," but rest assured that both the album and *The Wizard of Oz* enjoyed a little scratch thanks to increased sales from the sync story. Fortunately, the song also notes that money's "a gas"—especially when it's coming your way.

CHAPTER 55

DID KEITH MOON ROLL THAT ROYCE INTO A SWIMMING POOL?

WHY LET THE FACTS OF ONE CRAZY TWENTY-FIRST BIRTHDAY PARTY GET IN THE WAY OF A GOOD TIME—AND A GOOD STORY?

The best part about this story is that there is no single, definitive, agreed-upon account of what really happened. And since its perpetrator passed away in 1978, there never will be.

What we do know is that on the night of August 23, 1967, all sorts of mayhem occurred at the Holiday Inn in Flint, Michigan, at the hands of the Who and Herman's Hermits—and mostly thanks to Who drummer Keith Moon. The specific details, however, remain sketchy and contradictory, particularly the bit about whether or not Moon drove a luxury automobile into the hotel's empty swimming pool and, if so, what kind of car it was.

The uncertainty, of course, has led to *all* of the variations being reported and embraced over the years, and the night becoming one of the most notorious and enduring rock 'n' roll hotel-trashing tales.

Moon and the Who already had a reputation as a risky reservation for any hotel or motel, particularly Holiday Inns, the chain the group seemed to favor. The band that laid waste to its equipment at the end of its concerts had a similar appetite for destruction wherever it decided to bunk out for the night. Moon in particular liked to let off steam by chopping up hotel room furniture with a hatchet that he carried along, or by igniting cherry bombs and other munitions, sometimes lighting them and flushing them down the toilet. "Of course . . . we got thrown out of every hotel we ever stayed in," guitarist and chief songwriter Pete Townshend told Who biographer Dave Marsh. "It got to the point where they were asking five thousand dollars deposit to let us stay in even the shoddiest hotel."

Moon, however, was hardly contrite about it. "Boom! There goes another room," the drummer once told *Rolling Stone*. "What're you gonna do about it! Send us the bill. Fuck the expense. This is the attitude."

Moonie takes a seat on the bumper of a Rolls-Royce—no, not *that* Rolls-Royce. *Jim McCrary/Redferns/ Getty Images*

FOLLOWING PAGES:
The Who on the night of the great Flint Holiday Inn melee. It seems probable that they were louder than the headliners, Herman's Hermits. *Michael Ochs Archives/Getty Images*

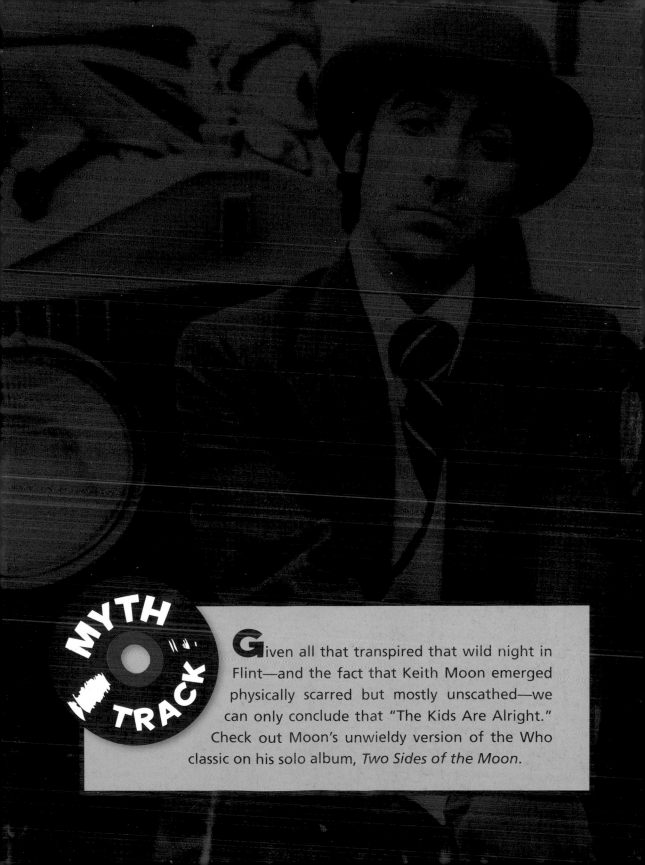

MYTH TRACK:

Given all that transpired that wild night in Flint—and the fact that Keith Moon emerged physically scarred but mostly unscathed—we can only conclude that "The Kids Are Alright." Check out Moon's unwieldy version of the Who classic on his solo album, *Two Sides of the Moon.*

Townshend, however, explained that the bad behavior was simply part and parcel with feeling lonely and alienated due to the grind of being on the road. Hotels, he said, "were a cold component in our lonely lives. We also appreciated their comfort, their clean sheets, the maids who cleaned, the people who brought food to our rooms, who prepared it, the people who made sure we had rooms in the first place. We're not stupid or ignorant. We were too young and spoiled to know any better at the time, so sometimes we made trouble."

And in Flint the trouble was a bit bigger than usual.

For starters, the Who were not happy to be out *opening* for Herman's Hermits, who were more commercially successful but less musically potent—and at the time starting to wane while the Who was clearly on the ascent. And the concert that night at Atwood Stadium was not well attended, even though Flint radio station WTRX was reputed to be the first in America to play the Who's music. Also, Moon, who was celebrating his twenty-first birthday, was drunk from the time the tour's private DC-7 landed in Flint and was in an advanced state of inebriation at the gig.

Nevertheless, all hands were in a partying spirit when they returned to the Holiday Inn on West Bristol Road. Decca Records, the Who's label, had sent drum-shaped cakes to select radio stations to commemorate the occasion, and the company had partnered with Premier Drums on a five-tier confection dedicated to Flint for the aftershow party, which was held in a banquet hall off the hotel lobby and attended by an estimated thirty to forty tour personnel, local DJs, and lucky fans.

Not surprisingly, things were a bit loud and rowdy. Moon even tried his requisite flushing of the firecrackers down the toilet in his room; they reportedly wouldn't go down the bowl, however, and he fled the room as porcelain flew like so much shrapnel. The party downstairs, meanwhile, raged until about midnight, when a hotel manager came in to shut it down.

Moon, by all accounts, was so upset that he hurled the birthday cake—at the wall, some say, or, according to others, at the Holiday Inn employee or a police officer providing security for the bash. Others began throwing food around the room, and the melee spilled out into the lobby and the hotel hallways. In some reports, a piano was obliterated. Fire extinguishers were taken from the wall and sprayed on cars in the parking lot and into the swimming pool, causing considerable damage. Moon, who was not sporting underwear, was also de-pantsed by some of his band mates and Herman (Peter Noone) and his Hermits, revealing both Moon's moon and his "sun."

Moon's attempts to escape the police, meanwhile, escalated an already good story to legendary status.

First came the car. According to varying eyewitness accounts, Moon ran into the parking lot, hopped into either (a) a Rolls-Royce, (b) a Cadillac, or

(c) a Lincoln Continental (the latter, according to Moon), which was either (a) unlocked or (b) broken into, then either (a) drove it into the pool or (b) released the parking brake and was helpless as the car rolled through a fence and into the crater. Moon also claimed that it was upon landing in the pool that he broke a front tooth on the vehicle's steering wheel.

Others, however, say neither car nor swimming pool were part of the night's high jinks. "The car thing didn't happen," said bassist John Entwistle, who was planning to write an autobiography with his own account of the night at the time of his death in 2002. "Keith didn't even really know how to drive, for starters. I don't know how that got to be part of the story. It's good, but it's not true."

Moon biographer Tony Fletcher, meanwhile, wrote in *Moon: The Life and Death of a Rock Legend* that "In his entire *life*, Keith Moon never drove a car into a swimming pool."

Moon, however, insisted during a 1972 interview with *Rolling Stone* that the car incident did indeed happen, though Fletcher contends that the drummer was purposely making up the story to embellish his reputation as a hellion.

There's no question that Moon did break a tooth, however. Entwistle said it occurred as Moon was trying to elude arrest after hitting an officer with some of the cake. Most accounts say Moon simply slipped on some icing that covered the floor. He was subsequently taken to a dentist in a police car, accompanied by Entwistle and Herman's Hermits bassist Karl Green for an emergency cap on the damaged chopper. He was apparently so drunk that Novocain was not needed. Some accounts claim he was then taken to the Genesee County Jail for a few hours, while others indicate he was never put behind bars.

The Who, meanwhile, took off for its next show—August 24 in Philadelphia—without the band's drummer, and Moon was whisked there later via private jet, "whimpering for about two days," Entwistle told biographer Johnny Black, from the residual pain of the dental procedure. The hotel damage has been reported at anywhere from $5,000 to $24,000. The Who was allegedly barred from the entire Holiday Inn chain after that, but that's more myth than reality as well, as the group stayed in other Holiday Inns during the same tour and on subsequent roadtrips, as well.

Sadly, the drummer was involved in a very real auto mishap a few years later. On January 4, 1970, a drunken Moon was fleeing the Red Lion pub in Hatfield, Hertfordshire, England, when he ran over and killed Neil Boland, a friend who also served as Moon's driver and bodyguard. Though it was ruled an accident and Moon was not charged, the incident haunted him until his own death on September 7, 1978, from a fatal mix of drugs and alcohol at the age of thirty-two. ✖

CHAPTER 56

DID KISS PUT A BIT OF THEMSELVES (LITERALLY) INTO THEIR COMIC BOOK?

WOULDN'T IT HAVE BEEN EASIER TO JUST CATCH SOME OF THE BLOOD GENE SIMMONS SPITS OUT DURING THE SHOWS?

Rock bands were not typical subjects for comic books in 1977. The Beatles were enough of a phenomenon to merit such treatment, but mostly it was a province for fake groups, such as the Archies or teeny-bop sensations like the Jackson 5.

KISS, however, was ripe for the comics world. The theatrical group's four dressed-up characters—The Demon (bassist Gene Simmons), Starchild (guitarist Paul Stanley), Spaceman (guitarist Ace Frehley), and Catman (drummer Peter Criss)—were ripped straight out of the cartoons and B-movies the band members favored. Some of its classic album covers—*Destroyer* and *Rock and Roll Over* in 1976, *Love Gun* in 1977, *Psycho Circus* in 1998, and *Sonic Boom* in 2009—have featured comic or graphic novel–style images of the band, while 1980's *Unmasked* sported a full-fledged comic strip. "We all grew up with comic books and superheroes and movie monsters and all of that," bassist Gene Simmons said. "That was very march part of our sensibility when we thought about the kind of band we wanted to be."

By 1977, the KISS concept was going over in a big way. After scoring commercial pay dirt and going gold with 1975's *Alive!* album and its hit single "Rock and Roll All Nite," KISS reeled off three consecutive platinum albums and added to the hit parade with "Shout It Out Loud," "Calling Dr. Love," "Christine Sixteen," "Love Gun," and the atypical ballad "Beth." The band was also raking in the merchandising dollars thanks to a devoted fan club known as the KISS Army that was eager to gobble up most anything that came its way.

Even the Kings of the Nighttime World need a business manager. KISS and theirs, Bill Aucoin (left), appeared on NBC in 1977.
AP Photo

Not surprisingly, others were looking to cash in on the KISS craze. That included Marvel Comics, home of Captain America, Iron Man, Spider-Man, Thor, the Avengers, and many other iconic heroes, some of which the men of KISS surely followed as youths. "It made perfect sense to do a KISS comic," Simmons said. "We were hot at the time—the hottest band in the land, right? That wasn't a joke or something we invented. We were. And when you're that hot, everybody wants a piece of you." Marvel included KISS in the May 1977 issue of its *Howard the Duck* series, then launched plans for a *KISS Super Special*.

And to make it even more special, the group members agreed to add a little extra ingredient to the ink that was being used to produce the comic book. As Simmons wrote in his 2001 autobiography *Kiss and Tell*: "[S]omeone came up with the idea of putting real blood in the ink. It wasn't me. . . . We got into a DC3, one of those big prop planes, and flew to Buffalo to Marvel's printing plant, where they pour the ink and make comic books. A notary public actually witnessed the blood being drawn."

The blood itself was drawn before a concert on Long Island. However, the "KISS Comic Book Contract" drawn up by the notary read: "This is to certify that KISS members, Gene Simmons, Ace Frehley, Paul Stanley and Peter Criss, have each donated blood which is being collectively mixed with the red ink to be used for the first issue of the Marvel/KISS comics. The blood was extracted on February 21st, 1977 at Nassau Coliseum and has been under guarded refrigeration until this day when it was delivered to Borden Ink plant in Depew, New York." KISS's trip to the plant, where they added the vials of blood to the ink, was photographed, of course, making the most of the publicity afforded by the gimmick.

An urban legend that popped up shortly after the bloodletting was that the ink was accidentally used to print an edition of *Sports Illustrated* rather than the *KISS Super Special*, but that's always been roundly denied by all concerned.

And Marvel's *KISS Super Special* was not the end of the group's comic book career. The company published a second KISS book in 1979. Almost two decades later, Image Comics published thirty-one issues of *Todd McFarlane's Kiss: Psycho Circus* starting in 1997, while Dark Horse launched a thirteen-issue KISS series in 2002 with X-Men writer Joe Casey (four of the stories became the graphic novel *Rediscovery*). The KISS Comics Group, meanwhile, was launched as a joint venture with Platinum Studio in early 2007; the first publication was based on the *Destroyer* album. And in 2011 the group signed on with IDW Publishing, home of the long-lived Archie series, for the *Archie Meets KISS* title. ✗

This is to certify that KISS members, Gene Simmons, Ace Frehley, Paul Stanley and Peter Criss, have each donated blood which is being collectively mixed with the red ink to be used for the first issue of the Marvel/KISS Comics. The blood was extracted on February 21st, 1977 at Nassau Coliseum and has been under guarded refrigeration until this day when it was delivered in an armored truck to the Borden Ink plant in Depew, New York.

Gene Simmons

AUCOIN
MANAGEMENT INC.

Ace Frehley

Paul Stanley

Peter Criss

Before me this 26th day of May, 1977, came Gene Simmons, Ace Frehley, Paul Stanley and Peter Criss, being known to me and known as the persons who signed the foregoing instrument and did so declare.

State of New York

County of Erie

Notary Public

MYTH TRACK

There's an outsized, comic book quality to everything KISS does, from its stage show to its album graphics to the big-riffing songs in its catalog. If the subject is comic books, though, we'll go with "God of Thunder" from 1976's *Destroyer* album. It's not about Thor, but it has that hammer-of-the-heavens quality you'd associate with any superhero tale.

CHAPTER 57

DID THIS ALTER-EGO GIVE PRINCE EXTRA STARR POWER?

WHAT DO U THINK?

"The main man behind everything." His Purple Highness onstage in 1985.
Michael Ochs Archives/ Getty Images

During the early and mid-1980s, few producers were as hot as Jamie Starr.

His run of hits included the first three albums by the Time, Sheila E's *The Glamorous Life*, and sets by Vanity 6 and Apollonia 6. You'd be hard-pressed to find a more consistently successful guy behind the control room glass.

You'd also be hard-pressed to find Jamie Starr.

Starr was a not-so-secret alter ego of one Prince Rogers Nelson—that would be Prince to you. While Prince took credit for the work he did under his own name, he adopted the Starr persona and a whole "organization" called the Starr Company as he put together his Minneapolis-based empire of acts. He explained to *Bass Player* magazine in 1999, many years after the Starr moniker had been retired, that he was "just getting tired of seeing my name. If you give away an idea, you still own that idea. In fact, giving it away strengthens it."

Prince—who was known to play most, if not all, of the instruments on the Starr-produced releases—and his minions certainly worked hard to make sure the Starr myth stayed strong during the time it was active, however.

When the Time released its self-titled debut album in 1981, frontman Morris Day, who was credited as Starr's co-producer, told *Rolling Stone*, "Jamie Starr is an engineer, the co-producer of our record. Of course he's real." Enterprising reporters, however, checked with the American Society of Composers, Authors and Publishers (ASCAP) to find out that some of the songs were registered to Prince, which Steve Fargnoli, Prince's manager

at the time, called "a filing mistake." Prince himself sought to "clear up a few rumors" with the *Los Angeles Times*, saying, "One, my real name is Prince. Two, I'm not gay. And three, I'm not Jamie Starr."

Vanity/Apollonia 6 member Brenda Bennett claimed that Starr "really exists. He's 68 or 69, a really cool cat. He's a Sammy Davis Jr. character, wears lots of gold and always has a suit on." And Fargnoli told a *Rolling Stone* reporter that Starr was "a reclusive maniac" who was "in and out of Minneapolis" and impossible to reach. But Minneapolis singer Sue Ann Carwell, a friend of Prince's, told the same writer, "Prince is Jamie Starr," while an anonymous associate added that "everybody knows [Prince is] the main man behind everything."

Conveniently, Bennett also noted in 1984, at the start of the *Purple Rain* world tour, that Starr had "retired from work behind the boards. He has remarked that, 'I had my time. It's up to you kids to do what you can with your music.'"

He hasn't been heard from since, and nobody has filed a missing persons report. ✖

MYTH TRACK

Besides production and engineering, Jamie Starr had a few songwriting credits. Among the most interesting is "Drive You Wild," a track that originally appeared on the 1982 *Vanity 6* album. It was later covered by the fun-loving Dave Grohl and his Foo Fighters and appeared on the tenth-anniversary edition of their 1997 sophomore album, *The Colour and the Shape*.

MORE ALTER(ED) EGOS AND ALBUM-CREDIT DISGUISES

Ryan Adams = Warren Peace, Sad Dracula, The Shit, Werewolph, and DJ Reggie

T Bone Burnett = Henry Coward

Eric Clapton = Derek Claptoe

Stewart Copeland = Klark Kent

Elvis Costello = The Imposter, Little Hands of Concrete, Howard Coward, and Napoleon Dynamite

Thomas Dolby = Booker I. Boffin

Bob Dylan = Blind Boy Grunt, Jack Frost, Bob Landy, Tendham Porterhouse, Robert Milkwood Thomas, Elston Gunnn, Sergei Petrov, Lucky Wilbury, and Boo Wilbury

Fleetwood Mac = Earle Vince & the Valiants

The Grateful Dead = McGannahan Skjellyfetti

Green Day = The Network (disputed)

David Grohl and Greg Ginn = Dale Nixon

George Harrison = Carl Harris, L'Angelo Mysterioso, Hari Georgeson, George Harrysong, George Harrisong, George O'Hara-Smith, Nelson Wilbury, and Spike Wilbury

Josh Homme = Carlo von Sexron and Baby Duck

Garth Hudson = Campo Malaqua

Mick Jagger/Keith Richards = The Glimmer Twins

Elton John = Ann Orson, Lord Choc Ice, William A. Bong, Reggae Dwight, and Frank N. Stein

Brian Jones = Elmo Lewis

John Lennon = Dr. Winston O'Boogie and Los Paranoias

Jeff Lynne = Otis Wilbury and Clayton Wilbury

Richard Manuel = Dick Handle

Paul McCartney = Paul Ramon, Apollo C. Vermouth, Bernard Webb, A. Smith, The Fireman, and Percy Thrillington

Freddie Mercury = Larry Lurex

Moby = Voodoo Child

Keith Moon = Kief Spoon and Baron von Moon

Graham Nash, Allan Clarke, and Tony Hicks = L. Ransford

Roy Orbison = Lefty Wilbury

Jimmy Page = S. Flavius Mercurius

Tom Petty = Charlie T. Wilbury Jr. and Muddy Wilbury

Billy Preston = Billy Presstud

The Rolling Stones = Nanker Phelge

Paul Simon = True Taylor, Jerry Landis, and Paul Kane

Phil Spector = Phil Harvey

Allen Toussaint = Naomi Neville

Pete Townshend = Bijou Drains

Steven Tyler/Joe Perry = The Toxic Twins

Eddie Vedder = Jerome Turner

Paul Westerberg = Pablo Louseorama and Grandpaboy

Jack White = "Doc" Gillis and John S. O'Leary (disputed)

Hank Williams = Luke the Drifter

Neil Young = Bernard Shakey and Joe Yankee

Frank Zappa = Lamarr Bruister, Stucco Homes, Obdwel'l X, Big Mother, Billy Dexter, and Mario Fuente

ACKNOWLEDGMENTS

It's no myth that Dan and Gary have been great friends for a very long time now, even though we're not really old enough to have done anything for a very long time—or so we like to think. We've shared work, war stories, life experiences, child- and pet-raising tips (not always one and the same), trips to Missouri Tigers football games, periodic sports rivalries, and occasional rounds of golf. This is the fourth one of these projects where we've been joined at the hip, and while it may be hard, it's always a pleasure.

We'd like to thank Dennis Pernu at Voyageur Press for signing us on for this book. Also to Adam Brunner for his photo research. We're also grateful for the work that all involved at Voyageur Press put into this.

Gary would like to extend great thanks to those I work with, and who, on a regular basis, gave me the leeway and latitude to work on *Rock 'n' Roll Myths*—even when they didn't know they were doing it: Jacquelyn Gutc, Julie Jacobson, Nicole Robertson, Steve Frye, and Glenn Gilbert at the *Oakland Press*; Marc Schneider, Jason Lipshutz, Tye Comer, Jessica Letkemann, and Bill Werde at *Billboard*/Billboard.com; Barbara Sharnak, Margaret Verghese, and the gang at the Pulse of Radio; Gayden Wren at the *New York Times* Syndicate; Brandon Geist and Kory Grow at *Revolver*; Tom Beaujour at *Guitar Aficionado*; Marcella S. Kreiter and John Hendel at UPI; Jon Ray, Brent Alberts, Jim O'Brien, and all at WCSX Detroit; Bob Madden, Brian Nelson, Eric Jensen, and Keith Hastings at WHQG (The HOG!) in Milwaukee; the dedicated crew of the Detroit Music Foundation and Detroit Music Awards; and a partridge in a pear tree. My gratitude also for support from friends, relatives, neighbors, and golf partners—too many to name without missing somebody important—but especially to my beloved Hannah, my dear Shari, and Liebe and Annie the wonder dogs, none of whom really care if Rod Stewart actually had his stomach pumped but gave me the latitude, and time, to try to find out.

Dan would like to thank Jody Mitori, Kevin C. Johnson, Barry Gilbert, and Evan Benn at the *St. Louis Post-Dispatch*; Ellen Futterman and Mike Sherwin at the *St. Louis Jewish Light*; Stefene Russell at *St. Louis Magazine*; and Steve Schenkel, Jeffrey Richard Carter, and the rest of the music department at Webster University. Thanks also to technical advisor and sounding board Jerome Peirick, plus-one pal Neal Thompson, the knowledgeable denizens of the Carosello Connection, everyone at MKI3K, and Chris Peimann, Sarah Samples, Amy Moorehouse, Angela Brown, Jesse Raya, and Steve Pohlman for service above and beyond the call. Love and thanks especially to the home team: my dear wife, Mary; great kids, Wolfgang, Eva, Stefan, and Hans; and my mom, Annie Durchholz. And of course, to Ute, too—good dog!

ABOUT THE AUTHORS

Gary Graff and Daniel Durchholz are co-authors of *Neil Young: Long May You Run: The Illustrated History* and co-editors of *MusicHound Rock: The Essential Album Guide*. In addition, Graff is an award-winning music journalist based in Detroit. He writes regularly for *Billboard* and Billboard.com, the *New York Times* Features Syndicate, Journal Register Company newspapers, *Revolver*, *Guitar Aficionado*, *Music Connection*, and other publications. He's also a correspondent for United Stations Radio Networks and provides music news reports for WCSX-FM in Detroit and WHQG-FM in Milwaukee. He is a co-founder of the Detroit Music Foundation and co-producer of the annual Detroit Music Awards. Graff has also published books about Bruce Springsteen and Bob Seger, and he is the founding editor of the MusicHound Essential Album Guide series.

Daniel Durchholz is a former editor at *Request and Replay* magazines and writes for the *St. Louis Post-Dispatch*, *St. Louis Magazine*, the *St. Louis Jewish Light*, and other publications. An adjunct assistant professor of music at Webster University, Durchholz lives in Wildwood, Missouri.

SOURCES

AUTHOR INTERVIEWS

Michael Anthony, Tom Araya, Brenda Bennett, Dewey Bunnell, Johnny Cash, Alice Cooper, Micky Dolenz, Russ Gibb, Jim Irsay, KISS (Gene Simmons and Paul Stanley), Lady Gaga, Thomas Lieber, Paul McCartney, Chris McKinney, Pink Floyd (David Gilmour and Nick Mason), Sting, Noel Paul Stookey, Donna Summer, Jimmy "Diamond" Williams, Weird Al Yankovic, and Peter Yarrow.

BOOKS AND MAGAZINES

Anderson, Chris. *Jagger Unauthorized*. New York: Delacorte Press, 1993.

Baird, Julia. *The Private John Lennon: The Untold History from His Sister*. Berkeley, CA: Ulysses Press, 2008.

Beatles, the. *The Beatles Anthology*. San Francisco: Chronicle Books, 2000.

Black, Johnny. *Eyewitness the Who: The Day-By-Day Story*. London: Carlton Books, 2001.

Bockris, Victor. *Keith Richards: The Biography*. New York: Poseidon Press, 1992.

Boese, Alex. *Hippo Eats Dwarf: A Field Guide to Hoaxes and other B.S.* New York: Mariner Books, 2006.

Bowie, Angela, with Patrick Carr. *Backstage Passes: Life on the Wild Side with David Bowie*. New York: Putnam, 1993.

Brown, Peter, and Steven Gaines. *The Love You Make: An Insider's Story of the Beatles*. New York: McGraw-Hill, 1983.

Bruce, Michael, with Billy James. *No More Mr. Nice Guy: The Inside Story of the Alice Cooper Group*. London: SAF Publishing, 1996.

Case, George. *Jimmy Page: Magus Musician Man*. New York: Hal Leonard, 2007.

Cole, Richard, and Richard Trubo. *Stairway to Heaven: Led Zeppelin Uncensored*. New York: HarperCollins, 1992.

Coleman, Ray. *Lennon: The Definitive Biography*. New York: HarperCollins, 1985.

Cooper, Alice, with Keith and Kent Zimmerman. *Alice Cooper, Golf Monster: A Rock 'n' Roller's 12 Steps to Becoming a Golf Addict*. New York: Crown Publishers, 2007.

Cross, Charles R. *Heavier Than Heaven: A Biography of Kurt Cobain*. New York: Hyperion, 2001.

——————. *Led Zeppelin: Shadows Taller Than Our Souls*. New York: It Books, 2009.

Davis, Francis. *The History of the Blues: The Roots, the Music, the People, from Charley Patton to Robert Cray*. New York: Hyperion, 1995.

Davis, Stephen. *Hammer of the Gods: The Led Zeppelin Saga*. New York: William Morrow, 1985.

Dowlding, William J. *Beatlesongs*. New York: Fireside, 1989.

Draper, Jason. *Prince: Chaos, Disorder, and Revolution*. New York: Backbeat Books, 2011.

Dylan, Bob. *Chronicles Volume One*. New York: Simon & Schuster, 2004.

Fiegel, Eddi. *Dream a Little Dream of Me: The Life of Cass Elliot*. London: Sidwick & Jackson, 2005.

Fletcher, Tony. *Moon: The Life and Death of a Rock Legend*. New York: Avon Books, 1999.

Fong-Torres, Ben. *Hickory Wind: The Life and Times of Gram Parsons*. New York: Pocket Books, 1991.

Goldman, Albert. *The Lives of John Lennon*. New York: William Morrow and Company, 1988.

Guralnick, Peter. *Feel Like Going Home: Portraits in Blues and Rock 'n' Roll*. New York: Outerbridge & Dienstfrey, 1971.

——————. *Searching for Robert Johnson*. London: Secker & Warburg, 1990.

Guralnick, Peter, Robert Santelli, Holly George-Warren, Christopher John Farley, eds. *Martin Scorsese Presents the Blues: A Musical Journey*. New York: HarperCollins, 2003.

Henderson, David. *Jimi Hendrix: Voodoo Child of the Aquarian Age*. New York: Doubleday, 1978.

Jackson, Laura. *Brian Jones: The Untold Life and Mysterious Death of a Rock Legend*. New York: Piatkus Books, 2009.

Jones, George, with Tom Carter. *I Lived to Tell It All*. New York: Villard, 1996.

Jones, Liz. *Purple Reign: The Artist Formerly Known as Prince*. New Jersey: Birch Lane Press, 1998.

Kane, Arthur. *I, Doll: Life and Death with the New York Dolls*. Chicago: Chicago Review Press, 2009.

Manson, Marilyn, with Neil Strauss. *The Long Hard Road Out of Hell*. New York: ReganBooks, 1998.

Marcus, Greil. *Dead Elvis*. New York: Doubleday, 1991.

Marsh, Dave. *Before I Get Old: The Story of the Who*. New York: St. Martin's Press, 1983.

McDermott, John, with Eddie Kramer. *Hendrix: Setting the Record Straight*. New York: Warner Books, 1992.

McDonough, Jimmy. *Tammy Wynette: Tragic Country Queen*. New York: Viking, 2010.

McNeil, Legs, and Gillian McCain. *Please Kill Me: The Uncensored Oral History of Punk*. New York: Grove Press, 1996.

Meyer, David N. *Twenty Thousand Roads: The Ballad of Gram Parsons and His Cosmic American Music.* New York: Villard, 2007.

Miles, Barry. *Paul McCartney: Many Years from Now.* New York: Henry Holt, 1997.

Murray, Charles Shaar. *Crosstown Traffic: Jimi Hendrix and the Rock 'n' Roll Revolution.* New York: St. Martin's Press, 1990.

Nilsen, Per. *DanceMusicSexRomance: Prince, the First Decade.* London: Firefly Publishing, 1999.

Osbourne, Ozzy, with Chris Ayers. *I Am Ozzy.* New York: Grand Central, 2009.

Patoski, Joe Nick. *Willie Nelson: An Epic Life.* New York: Black Bay Books, 2008.

Philips, John. *Papa John.* New York: Dolphin Books, 1986.

Rawlings, Terry. *Brian Jones: Who Killed Christopher Robin?: The Truth Behind the Murder of a Rolling Stone.* London: Boxtree, 1994.

Richards, Keith, with James Fox. *Life.* New York: Little, Brown, 2010.

Roth, David Lee. *Crazy from the Heat.* New York: Hyperion, 1997.

Sanchez, Tony. *Up and Down with the Rolling Stones.* New York: William Morrow, 1979.

Savage, Jon. *England's Dreaming: Anarchy, Sex Pistols, Punk Rock, and Beyond.* New York: St. Martin's Press, 1992.

Shelton, Robert. *No Direction Home: The Life and Music of Bob Dylan.* New York: Beech Tree Books, 1986.

Shotton, Pete, and Nicholas Schaffner. *John Lennon: In My Life.* New York: Thunder's Mouth Press, 1994.

Simmons, Gene. *Kiss and Make-Up.* New York: Crown, 2002.

Slick, Grace, with Andrea Cagan. *Somebody to Love? A Rock-and-Roll Memoir.* New York: Grand Central Publishing, 1998.

Smith, Danyel. "Tupac Shakur" in *The Vibe History of Hip Hop,* ed. Alan Light. New York: Three Rivers Press, 1999.

Sweet, Brian. *Steely Dan: Reelin' in the Years.* London: Omnibus Press, 1994.

Taraborrelli, J. Randy. *Michael Jackson: The Magic and the Madness.* New York: Birch Lane Press, 1991.

Various. *Guitar World Presents Kiss.* New York: Hal Leonard Books, 1997.

————. *Jack White: The Full Story of a 21st Century Icon.* London: Uncut, 2011.

————. *Mojo Classic: Led Zeppelin & the Story of 1969: The Ultimate Collector's Edition.* London: Bauer London Lifestyle, 2009.

————. *Pink Floyd: The Ultimate Music Guide.* London: Uncut, 2011.

————. *Punk: The Whole Story.* London: Dorling Kindersley, 2006.

————. *The Who: The Ultimate Music Guide.* London: Uncut, 2011.

Weiner, Sue, and Lisa Howard. *The Rolling Stones A to Z.* New York: Evergreen, 1983.

White, Timothy. *Rock Lives: Profiles and Interviews.* New York: Henry Holt, 1990.

Wohlin, Anna. *The Murder of Brian Jones.* London: Blake Publishing, 2001.

Wynette, Tammy, with Joan Dew. *Stand by Your Man.* New York: Simon & Schuster, 1979.

Zappa, Frank, with Peter Occhiogrosso. *The Real Frank Zappa Book.* New York: Poseidon Press, 1989.

Zimmer, David, and Henry Diltz. *Crosby, Stills & Nash: The Biography.* New York: Da Capo Press, 2000.

PERIODICALS AND WEBSITES

About.com

Allhiphop.com

Beliefnet.com

Des Moines Register

Entertainment Weekly

The Guardian

IMDB.com

Mojo

New York Times

NME

Playboy

Q

Rolling Stone

Snopes.com

Spin

The Telegraph

Twitter

Uncut

Washington Post

Zappa Wiki Jawaka

FILMS AND TELEVISION

Broomfield, Nick, dir. *Kurt and Courtney.* Fox Lorber, 1999.

Hennig, Gandulf, dir. *Gram Parsons: Fallen Angel.* Rhino, 2006.

Mason, Anthony. Keith Richards interview, *CBS Sunday Morning.* CBS, October 24, 2010.

Scorsese, Martin, dir. *No Direction Home: Bob Dylan.* Paramount, 2005.

Winfrey, Oprah. *Michael Jackson Talks . . . to Oprah: 90 Primetime Minutes with the King of Pop.* ABC, February 10, 1993.

INDEX